Gill Sarre

POWERFUL
PRESENTATIONS

POWERFUL PRESENTATIONS

50 ORIGINAL IDEAS FOR MAKING A REAL IMPACT

Jöns Ehrenborg and John Mattock

First published in 1993

The masculine pronoun has been used throughout this book. This stems from a desire to avoid ugly and cumbersome language, and no discrimination, prejudice or bias is intended.

Apart from any fair dealing for the purposes of research or private study, or criticism or review, as permitted under the Copyright, Designs and Patents Act, 1988, this publication may only be reproduced, stored or transmitted, in any form or by any means, with the prior permission in writing of the publishers, or in the case of reprographic reproduction in accordance with the terms of licences issued by the Copyright Licensing Agency. Enquiries concerning reproduction outside those terms should be sent to the publishers at the undermentioned address:

Kogan Page Limited
120 Pentonville Road
London N1 9JN

© Jöns Ehrenborg and John Mattock, 1993

British Library Cataloguing in Publication Data

A CIP record for this book is available from the British Library.

ISBN 0 7494 1164 3

Typeset by Books Unlimited (Nottm), Sutton-in-Ashfield, NG17 1AL
Printed in England by Clays Ltd, St Ives plc.

Contents

Introduction	7
1 What's happening in your listener's head?	9
2 What will stick in your listener's mind? *Pictures!*	23
3 What else will stick in your listener's mind? *Stories and emotions!*	43
4 How can you draw your listeners into your story?	55
5 Can you really change your listener's beliefs?	73
6 How should you build and deliver your argument?	85
Synopsis	109
Afterword	113
Appendices	115

Introduction

> If I want to succeed in guiding a human being towards a settled goal, I must first find him where he is, and start just there.... To help a person, I must of course understand more than he does, but above all I must understand what he understands.... If I still want to show how much I know, it is because I am vain and proud.... All true helpfulness starts with humility towards the human being I want to help, and accordingly I must understand that helping is not the wish to rule but the wish to serve.
>
> *Sören Kierkegaard*

Much of this book is devoted to influencing other people – which we hope is usually in order to help them.

The book is for you if you ever feel that some of your presentations are stale, or if you doubt sometimes that your message has gone across powerfully.

The chapters can be read in sequence, as a kind of seminar. We strongly suggest you give a little time and thought to the exercises. Alternatively, you can put the book on your shelf, and take it down for a shot when next you are preparing an important presentation.

Our main focus has been the full, prepared presentation to a captive audience. Much of what we offer, however, would be equally relevant to a one-to-one encounter with your bank manager. Our reference point throughout is your audience. We begin with them, and their state of mind as you begin your presentation.

1

What's happening in your listener's head?

A dialogue, that's what.
From the moment you start your presentation, one part of your listener's mind is asking questions:

> Is this message for me?

> Can I believe in the contents of this message?

> Is this speaker 'one of us'?

Another part of his mind is receiving the questions, paying attention to your messages, and trying to find the answers there.

In this chapter we will take the three questions in turn, and consider what you, the speaker, must do to secure the answers:

> Yes

> Yes

> Yes

QUESTION ONE
IS THIS MESSAGE FOR ME?

To paraphrase Abe Lincoln: many people are fairly gullible quite a lot of the time.

This fact keeps advertising agencies in business.

The agencies' clients demand proof that their money is being well spent:

---

* Another part again is wool-gathering – gazing out of the window, thinking about his love-life, worrying about his waistline. Later in this book we suggest ways to make sure this doesn't happen *too* much.

- ❏ 'Is our cat food selling better since we adopted the new slogan?'
- ❏ 'Have more people opened accounts with our bank since we doubled our spend on TV promotion?'

If the answer is 'no', the campaign is scrapped.

So most of the advertising messages you know well are *successful* messages. They are printed and broadcast over and over again because they really do persuade people to buy the product or the service.

Now consider how many of these messages are built on an absurd premise: *that the advertiser knows about you personally*. We hear:

Yummikins...because your cat deserves it!

A higher interest rate deposit account, where your money works harder for you!

Of course, we all know that the money in a deposit account is working largely for the benefit of the bank; and as for the cat, he doesn't 'deserve' anything, since he's never done anything for anybody but himself.

Yet reason counts for little in these cases. Much more important is audience identification – the process by which a listener says: 'Ah! This message is for me! I'll sit up and take notice!' The key expressions are '*your* cat' and '*your* money'.

If five people are watching TV, and four of them are non-catowners (even cat haters), they will not object intellectually or emotionally to the message '...because your cat deserves it'. They will simply ignore the message, as 'nothing to do with me'.

The fifth, a catowner, feels (not thinks, just *feels*) that the warm, sincere, gently humorous voice coming from the TV speaker is addressing him or her personally: 'I am being told that my cat deserves it...must look out for it next time I go to the supermarket...'

As for the banking services ad, consider how many of our five viewers would perk up and pay attention if the message '...where your money works harder for you' were replaced by 'where money works harder'. Their thoughts might be: 'Works harder, does it? So what? Has anybody got anything to say that might be of interest to me?'

Which has the power:

> **Your country needs you**

or

> **This country needs soldiers?**

Are we chilled by

> **Big brother is watching you**

or

> **Big brother is watching every citizen?**

Of course, not all advertising is so unsubtle as to use 'you', 'your' and 'yours' this blatantly. Yet all successful advertising achieves this goal somehow: the individual who is expected to remember and act on the message is first made to feel that it is directed at him personally. Otherwise, NO SALE.

Next time you watch a battery of ads, on TV or in the cinema, watch for the trick or device in each case. How does the advertiser involve the individual viewer? (Often it is by means of a joke. If a viewer/listener/reader smiles or laughs at an advertising message, the bond is very strong: 'This makes *me* laugh; it fits *my* sense of humour.')

What this means to you

When you are preparing a campaign of persuasion for an audience of one or fifty, you have a great advantage over the creative department in an advertising agency.

They have to make educated guesses at the inclinations of millions, and then hope to capture their attention.

With a smaller, more specific target, you can shape your message to suit perfectly the watching and listening mind:

Wake up! Pay attention! This means you! Yes, you!

I know you're interested, because I've done my homework.

If you fail to use that advantage, you will never persuade your listeners.

Cocktail Party Exercise

Position yourself on the opposite side of a crowded room from somebody whose name you know – Peter Fletcher, let's say.

Start a conversation with somebody about a safe and light-hearted topic – rose gardening, for example. Choose something you know Peter Fletcher is interested in.

The other two dozen people in the room will soon be similarly occupied, and the air filled with an inchoate chatter. No two consecutive words will be audible from more than three paces away.

In a clear voice, but without shouting, say to your partner: 'Of course, Peter Fletcher is the man to talk to about roses'.

The people in the middle of the room will notice nothing. Beyond the throng, Peter Fletcher will stop whatever he is doing, look your way, smile, and mouth 'Talking about me?'

The most dangerous subject in the world

...is the subject where *you* are a great expert or a great enthusiast. You can so easily begin to drone on about it for your own satisfaction or pleasure.

Your listener will sense this, and his internal dialogue will proceed like this:

Q: Is this message for me?

A: Obviously not. This bloke's talking to himself.

QUESTION TWO
CAN I BELIEVE IN THE CONTENTS OF THIS MESSAGE?

When you meet a dog, and the dog sniffs your hand, he is making sure you are not a chicken, a lion, or another dog who is about to challenge him.

When you are setting out to present your case, you must let your audience sniff your hand – to make sure you are not a fanatic, a liar or a clown.

Your personal credibility comes before the plausibility of your message. Before you give your audience something new to think about, you have to establish your credentials as a source of good, true, wholesome ideas. Or at least of accurate and useful information.

> 'At this point in the relationship, you have to provide us with a token of your sincerity,' Pogodin said...
>
> The invitation dangled before Lewinter. He considered his laminated ID card, his MIT faculty card, his passport. But he knew that none of these would get him on the eight o'clock plane to Moscow.
>
> 'Look', he said, 'I could give you the formula for the trajectory of one of the decoys in a MIRV. You can cable it to Moscow. Surely there must be someone there who can vouch for its value.'
>
> Without a flicker of expression, Pogodin offered the green notebook to Lewinter.
>
> 'Do you need a pen?' he asked politely.
>
> *Robert Littell,*
> *The Defection of A J Lewinter*

The best, truest, most wholesome ideas are the ones that your audience can check against what they already know or believe or feel. If your first statement matches what they find in their own mental wardrobe, they will approve of it. They won't object. They won't say 'What a waste of time. He's telling me something I already know'. Rather, they will smile and nod.

When you see that signal, your listener is telling you:

'I have checked this statement against what I know to be true; I find that it agrees; I am now prepared to believe the next thing you tell me'. Once they have started nodding, it will be easier to keep them nodding.

If you have established yourself already as a source of good, true, wholesome facts, your key message, when you deliver it, will go through the Green Channel – be more easily imported into your audience's mind.

'He's right, you know. I had the same experience myself!'

'How many times have I said the same thing?'

'At last! Somebody to back up what I've been saying all these years!'

'True, true. How very true!'

What this means to you

Before you try to influence your audience, win their trust.

Give them a piece of information they already have; suggest an opinion they already hold; express an emotion they already feel.

When somebody lends you a book

...is he more likely to say:

(a) 'This is really good; it encapsulates a lot of things I've felt for a long time',

or

(b) 'This is really good; it propounds a lot of ideas I disagreed with before, and it's forced me to admit I was wrong'?

The experienced persuader often goes one step further to establish himself as honest: he admits to one fact which clearly militates *against* the general thrust of his argument.

He does not damage his case by expressing some *new* argument against it. No, he tells his audience something they already know, or can see for themselves.

That way he gets a *double* nod:

This speaker has told me something I already know, so I will nod in agreement; he has shown himself to be fair, honest and a little bit audacious, so I will nod in approval.

What this means to you

At an everyday level, you can win a lot of credibility with your listener if you say:

I'll readily admit that our prices are above average...

Of course, there's no guarantee of success attached to the course of action I'm about to recommend...

Our competitor's product has many excellent features...

We made a mistake. In fact, I made a mistake...

All of this is building up to answer the next question in your audience's mind...

QUESTION THREE
IS THIS SPEAKER 'ONE OF US'?

You have heard people preparing their arguments, saying: 'This will surprise them, you'll see. They'll really have to sit up and take notice when I deliver this bombshell!'

What it really means is 'This idea will be rejected straight away'.

Your audience will not easily accept ideas which are in direct conflict with their prejudices. You must shape your arguments so as to achieve confluence with the direction of their thinking.

We consider the technique in more detail later; for the moment, we simply say that your job is a thousand times easier if you help your listeners to see that you are one of them. And do it at the very start of your presentation.

TELL them you are one of them:

> Ich bin ein Berliner
>
> *John F Kennedy*

The Kennedy example is clear. It mattered little that he was manifestly not a Berliner, nor that some members of his audience knew a *berliner* as a particular sort of doughnut. The response was warm and enthusiastic – from a beleaguered people who were very ready to believe that they had a powerful ally in the White House.

What this means to you

You can achieve a lot by saying:

> *I understand that you are unhappy about the fall in your share value. I am a major shareholder in this company myself.*

> *I have given a lot of thought to this investment programme. As an engineer myself, I know the frustration of trying to get results with limited resources.*

TELL them you're not using tricks to bamboozle them:

> ... Rude am I in my speech,
> And little blest with the set phrase of peace...
> I will a round unvarnished tale deliver...
>
> *Shakespeare's Othello*

WHAT'S HAPPENING IN YOUR LISTENER'S HEAD?/17

In fact, Othello commands all the 'smooth parts of speech', and everybody at the Venetian court must have admired his oratory.

Yet when he delivers this promise of straight, forthright dealing, his listeners settle themselves to receive a 'round unvarnished tale', reassured that they are in no danger of being manipulated.

What this means to you

Avoid the old cliché:

> Unaccustomed as I am to public speaking...

but try one of these:

> Now it's better to let the facts speak for themselves...

> When I look at the complexity of this issue, I get dizzy. But I have found it helpful to think about the simple basics...

> I wouldn't dream of trying to convince you of something you know to be untrue...

TELL them you are not a privileged and special person:

> When I first came to this land, I was not a wealthy man.
>
> *American folk song*

A friend of ours recalls a visit to his school by a distinguished Old Boy – Field Marshall Lord Montgomery of Alamein. Monty had chosen to hand out copies of his autobiography as prizes:

> There are two kinds of book: good books and rotten books. This is a good book. I wrote it.

Every schoolboy in the audience had suffered from being forced to read 'rotten' books (heavy books with no action, mainly), and received Monty's message: 'I am just like you'.

The message was reinforced by the choice of language – simple, clear schoolboy stuff.

Nineteen little words that have stuck in our friend's mind for 30 years. A very good result.

> ### What this means to you
>
> Try something like these in your presentation:
>
> *My grandfather, a carpenter, gave me a very important piece of advice...*
>
> *When I was putting in my time on the assembly line at our factory down the road here...*
>
> *I'm pleased to note that the apple pie in the canteen is just as substantial as it was in my younger days...*

Everybody can manage at least the very beginning of one of Shakespeare's great speeches: 'Friends, Romans, countrymen...'; yet few consider how much Mark Antony achieves in these first three words.

Throughout his speech he returns again and again to the themes:

- I am myself, and not playing any role;
- I am a plain blunt man;
- I have no enemies, everybody trusts me;
- I will put simple facts before you; and
- You know all this anyway.

There is a huge gulf between the speaker – a patrician senator – and the audience – the stinking Roman mob. This makes it all the more essential for Mark Antony to hammer home his message:

> **Forget the others; I'm on your side!**

THE INTERNATIONAL ARENA

At the end of each chapter or major section, we shall consider what additional factors come into play when you, as speaker, are working across a culture gap.

We have studied at first hand the things that happen to communication when it 'goes international', and enjoyed the experience very much.

We aim to avoid academic models of cross-cultural transactions, although we have certainly made use of them ourselves in interpreting what we see around us. More useful to the general reader – the business person who travels – is advice on practical matters.

For example, when you are introducing yourself, your company or your product – in a presentation or at an informal gathering – there is a moment of danger. All these names are familiar to you, the speaker; you have spoken them many thousands of times – *within your home culture*.

Within your home culture, however, the combinations of sounds you make are easily heard and understood and stored in the mind of your listener. So you are free to drop your voice a little and speak quickly – which many people do out of a sort of modesty.

This is no good in the international arena. Imagine being introduced to a Japanese businessman, who drops his eyes, lowers his voice to a mumble, and says: 'How do you do? Hiromichiodagirimasayumacorporationhiro'. Do you feel competent to continue the conversation? We do not need to dwell on the difficulty, 20 minutes later, of saying: 'I'm sorry, I didn't catch the name of your company'.

Even within Europe, similar strained moments are possible between Swedish and French, English and Spanish, Hungarians and everyone. The only solution is to *slow down*, rather than speeding up, and provide plenty of additional markers in what you say.

Our Japanese meant: 'My name is Odagiri, Hiromichi Odagiri, and I work for the Masayuma Corporation. Please call me Hiro.'

If our advice here seems obvious, that's fine. Yet we have often found that people have trouble putting common sense into practice.

Our general advice for dealing across cultures is simple:

Be flexible

Everybody should modify his behaviour – and his presentations – when he is meeting foreigners, on their territory or on his own.

The best way to get good service is to be a good customer.

Be attentive

We also challenge the reader really to keep his wits about him at such times; it is vital to continue developing your own personal *model*: 'In this other culture, what lies in the background to produce this behaviour?'

The best way to get answers is to ask questions.

Be yourself

And we comfort the reader by stressing: 'at all times, stay rooted in what you are'.

OUR SAMPLE

We have addressed ourselves chiefly to a north-west European audience, bearing North America in mind.

Such a focus was necessary: almost any observation made about culture is bound to be a *relative* observation – people in Culture A do the opposite from those in Culture B, or do the same thing more intensely – so some stable reference point was required.

We cast our net a little wider for examples where wider examples seemed right, but given our Swedish–English axis, please expect a preponderance of examples from that world.

SUMMARY

Briefly, this chapter was all about establishing trust.

As speakers we need to know if the listener is trusting us – whether the audience is prepared yet for the important thing we want to say.

This is partly why we depend so much on reciprocal grunts ('Yes...go on...quite!...I see....Mmhmm') and sub-verbal agreement signals (smiles, nods, raised eyebrows).

Some cultures – the Finns, for example – give very few such signals. Trying to convince a Finn of something new can be rather unnerving: you don't know if the Green Channel is open or not.

For an Englishman, running training courses in the Nordic Zone can be a little unnerving. A small minority of the more outgoing brethren give you all your feedback, while the rest seem to be quietly gazing in your general direction, reserving judgment.

Conversely, a Japanese who nods repeatedly and says 'Yes...yes...yes...' is probably not signalling acceptance of your argument, but just telling you that he has heard and understood your words. Equally disturbing if you are not prepared for it.

An American colleague, living and working in Switzerland, was uncomfortable for weeks. It seemed that everybody was emitting a series of 'Ja, ja...Ja, ja' noises when he spoke to them. They were just signalling 'I'm listening'. The man from Pittsburgh was receiving a different message: 'yah, yah...yah, yah....I'm bored, and I don't really believe you'.

What this means to you

...if they're a bit lively

In personal conversation, if you're getting more vociferous signals than you are used to, you will tend to feel:

> This person is pushy/aggressive/ill-mannered/in poor control of himself.

Fight that feeling. Remember, it probably means that he is finding you a bit cool, and is waiting for you to open up a bit too.

When you are making a presentation, just relax and enjoy it. We have never heard of a speaker who preferred a dead audience to a responsive one.

...if they're a bit passive

One-to-one, you will probably find yourself adjusting your own volume control knob – downwards. You should try to, otherwise you could be grating on your partner's nerves.

He will give you clear signals of encouragement – smiles, laughter – if he is enjoying your boisterousness.

The same is true of your audience at a presentation: if you stay alert to them as you speak, you will adjust accordingly. Let yourself rip from time to time, and you'll be remembered.

If you are not sure that they're responding to your message, ask them a direct question:

> Are you in broad agreement so far?;

or

> Now before I move on to the next stage, could I ask you if it's clear/relevant to you so far?

Those were Yes–No questions. To really check their involvement, ask *open* questions:

> Where might this information be useful to you?

or

> How will this proposal affect your job?

2

What will stick in your listener's mind?

PICTURES!

Once more, the three questions in your listener's mind as he tunes in to your presentation:

- ❏ Is this message for me?
- ❏ Can I believe in the contents of this message?
- ❏ Is this speaker 'one of us'?

Assuming that you and your message chalk up three YESes, and that you have the attention and the trust of the audience, we can now address a question crucial to you, as presenter.

HOW DOES YOUR AUDIENCE REMEMBER?

The answer:

> In pictures

Some speakers – failed politicians, bad teachers, starving salesmen – choose to suppose that an audience will remember everything they say. Hopeless!

People remember *impressions*

Cast your mind back to a speech or lecture or presentation you have sat through (and it doesn't really matter how long ago it was). How much can you recall? How much detail? How many numbers? Dates? Names? Can you actually bring back to mind the words the speaker used?

Now some rather different questions to answer from memory: was the speaker a man or a woman? Attractive? What colour hair?

Standing or sitting? A lot of arm-waving, or a static performance? Formal or relaxed? Happy or sad?

Your memories of impressions at the sub-verbal level can be surprisingly strong.

People remember **visual stimuli**

To take an example nearer the present, can you remember either of the names of the authors of this book? We don't flatter ourselves....

But do you remember the colour of the cover of the book?

People remember **analogies and symbols**

One of the present authors had an interest in Irish history, and developed a 60-minute illustrated lecture on the subject, full of Irish jokes, Irish sentiment, exciting Irish battles and romantic Irish heroes. The audiences, from all over continental Europe, stayed awake throughout. Often, the speaker would meet the group later in their seminar, and be greeted with: 'We all very much enjoyed your speech about Scotland'.

Yet all the audiences at the lecture remembered the Shamrock – the little plant with a triple leaf, which is now the Irish national emblem and the logo of Aer Lingus. Tradition has it that Saint Patrick used it 1500 years ago as a way of explaining to simple peasants the rather complex doctrine of the Holy Trinity. He used it as a prop or mnemonic device. As a *visual aid*.

Once your words leave your lips, they are out of your control. Speaking a sentence to an audience is like throwing a rock into a pond: the splash is heard and felt, and the ripples spread, bobbing

WHAT WILL STICK IN YOUR LISTENER'S MIND?/25

twigs and leaves about, bending the plants at the rim, stirring up the mud on the bottom. Your words set off chain reactions – unconscious connotations and personal associations – in your listeners' minds. Your meaning is soon distorted or lost.

This effect is well recognized, and the basis of parlour pastimes and TV game shows – Chinese whispers, the marriage game, and so on.

Moreover, if ever you have been misquoted in a newspaper you will know the feeling of exasperation: 'wasn't that bloody reporter paying any attention to what I said?'

Words are very easy to forget.

What this means to you

When you design your next presentation, or when you are dusting off an old favourite, you must recognize that general **impressions**, strong **visual stimuli**, and potent **analogies and examples** are the keys to your audience's memory bank.

Use the keys.

Are there some rules you can learn and apply? Are there ways to make the most of your listener's imperfect memory? Yes, indeed there are.

First, and most basic:

Emulate Saint Patrick

He knew that people remember what they have seen with their eyes and in their minds – *not* the words they have heard or read.

One sure way to make a moment more memorable is to attract and surprise the eyes of your audience.

WHAT IS NOT A VISUAL AID?

A table of production output estimates, photographed onto a 35 mm slide from a company report, is not a visual aid. A system diagram of a telephone exchange, borrowed from the wall of the engineers' training school, is not a visual aid. An overhead transparency of the latest inspirational speech by the Sales Vice President is not a visual aid.

We estimate that 90 per cent of what is shown to audiences during business presentations is a waste of effort – to say nothing of film, flip-chart paper, acetate foils and felt-tip pens.

If your so-called visual aid does not help the audience to see, understand, and remember the point you are making,

Replace it or leave it out.

True quotations

I know you can't actually see the figures on this slide; I had quite a lot of detail to squeeze in. I'll read it out to you....

My son always jokes when he sees me packing for a business trip: "Good old Dad – 100 OPM!" He means 100 Overheads Per Minute....

I found this cartoon in a magazine I was reading. It hasn't really got a lot to do with my theme today, which as you will remember is 'Leadership', but I found it amusing....

Why not bung another graph in – it can't do any harm....

Oh, yes it can. A bad visual, or a visual badly used, will do serious damage to your reputation as a presenter. Your audience will retain a strong visual memory of you, performing badly.

What this means to you

Not a lot – yet. The rest of this chapter tells you how to distinguish between good and bad visual aids.

When you have read it, you will know which visuals should be dumped...quickly! Before you are tempted to use them again!

WHAT IS ALMOST A VISUAL AID?

The people who make personal computers, and desktop publishing software, want you to buy their goods. They say to you:

- Look at these **graphs/ pie charts/ histograms**!
- Aren't they **professional/ impressive/ expensive-looking**!
- Now your customers will **buy your product/** the board will **accept your proposal/** your boss will **give you a pay-rise**!

We have grave doubts about all this. We say:

- Look! They're **all the same**!
- Aren't they **dull**!
- Now we know that you can work a PC keyboard. **Big deal**!

We accept that charts, diagrams and similar conventional representations can be helpful when you are *explaining* a point, but they do not stimulate the imagination, or lodge themselves in the memory.

What this means to you

Ask yourself sincerely: do you want your idea to be remembered? If the answer is no, then illustrate it in the same style as all the other ideas in all the other presentations your audience is watching these days. Use the graphics package. Then you will be one of the crowd:

```
o   o   o   o   o   o   o   o   o
+   +   +   +   +   +   +   +   +
^   ^   ^   ^   ^   ^   ^   ^   ^
```

On the other hand, you could be audacious! Decide to be memorable! Turn the clock back! Be primitive! **Make your own visual in your own style**!

```
o   o   o   o   o       o   o   o
+   +   +   +   +       +   +   +
^   ^   ^   ^   ^       ^   ^   ^
```

HOW TO MAKE A USEFUL VISUAL AID

Accept that your first idea will not be your best

No artist can say: 'I will consult my muse over coffee at 11 o'clock, and start painting at ten past'. Why should you be different?

When you are translating from the world of concepts to the world of visual representation, you should be prepared to discard your first few efforts.

Even if your objective is just a functional, attractive diagram, to support a commonsense argument, you are setting out on a creative journey.

Give the creative process a chance

Jot a few ideas down with pencil and paper on your notepad. Put them aside and do something else for a while. Jot a few new ideas down with fat felt-tips on a white-board. Set them aside and go for lunch. Modify your earlier ideas, using different coloured inks and paper. Go home and sleep on it. The quiet periods are known variously as 'getting some distance', 'referring the matter to your sub-conscious', or 'incubating'.

The changes in colour and material are a good way to lighten up and stimulate the right-hand side of your brain – where all the visualizing takes place. Drawing in wet sand with a piece of driftwood is highly recommended.

Three creative ten-minute sessions, with your right brain running free, will produce more potential goodies than a solid hour stuck in a rut on the left side.

Use another person to get your creative juices running

Sit down with a friend over a beer, and talk it through – *making sure you have a ball-point pen and plenty of beer mats to draw on*. One of the beer mats might just become the heart of the company's next million-dollar advertising campaign.

Can you imagine explaining the 4-stroke internal combustion engine to a 12-year-old child without something to draw with?

Simplify, simplify, simplify

Your key drawing or diagram must be designed as an aid to memory. If there is too much detail, the mind of your audience will flush away all the peripheral information, *together with your central point*:

> You give me too much to remember, so I will remember nothing.

Check that the draft means what you want it to mean

Choose a friend, relation or colleague who knows little about the message you are trying to transmit. Show him the draft of your visual with very little comment – just enough context so he can try to grasp the meaning of the thing. Then ask him to talk about what he sees and how he interprets it. Listen carefully.

If your visual aid is transmitting the wrong message, or is ambiguous or impenetrable, don't try to defend it or justify it. Take it away and modify it. Perhaps better, take it away and scrap it.

Keep revising your draft

If the idea seems to work, play around with the colours, dimensions, spacing. Turn it upside down and back to front. If there is lettering, change from lower case to UPPER CASE or vice-versa.

One version will seem stronger and clearer than the others. Select that one for final production. (If you then pass it on to your company's drawing office, or graphics department, insist that they produce the piece according to your specifications, and do not 'improve' things when your back is turned. Most of these people have never made a presentation in their lives.)

Check that the final version is legible

If you are going to use an OHP slide, you should be able to prop the acetate foil on a shelf, against a white wall, and read it from 4 metres. Otherwise, when you project it on the screen, the people in the back row of the auditorium will suffer eye strain and irritation.

Even better, ask a colleague to read it on the shelf. Since you already know what it says, you could probably convince yourself that it is legible at any distance.

High contrast is best – black or dark blue on white or yellow; white or yellow reversed out of black or dark blue. Red is dramatic at close range, on the printed page, but it is less striking over distance.

COLOUR RULES IN HERALDRY

In the Middle Ages, a knight in full armour, visor and all, was unrecognizable to friend or enemy. So he wore a surcoat, with his armorial bearings – his coat of arms.

It was vital that the markings should be discernible at a great distance; longbows were powerful and accurate. This demand for survival, combined with an empirical understanding of the visual power of contrast, led to certain rules in heraldry.

There are five principal colours in heraldry: red, blue, black, green and purple. There are two metals: gold (yellow) and silver (white). On a metal ground, only a colour could be used. On a coloured ground, only a metal. Never metal on metal, nor colour on colour. *Contrast* !

Translating words into diagrams

When I joined the company, I found an atmosphere of mistrust and recrimination:

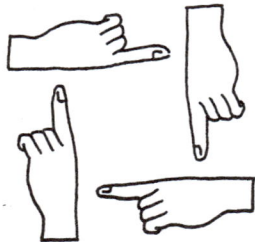

If we are to survive, we must support each other as a team:

Translating numbers into diagrams

...20 per cent of the people in the world consume 80 per cent of the world's resources

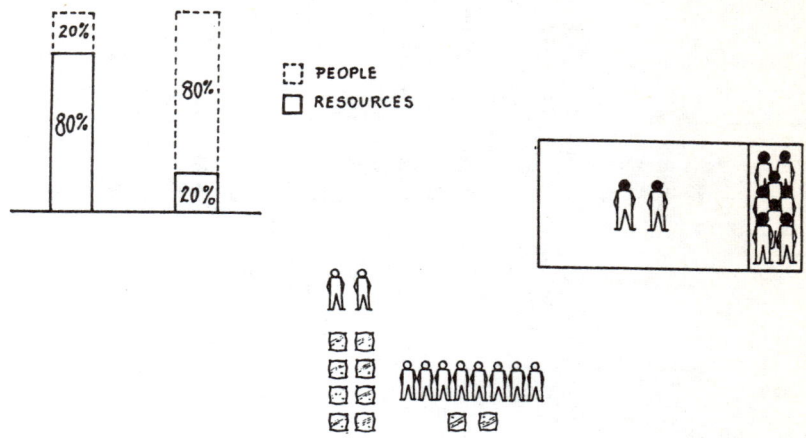

Choose your favourite from among these. Finally, it's subjective.

Is this legible?

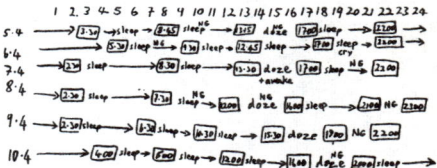

Is this clear?

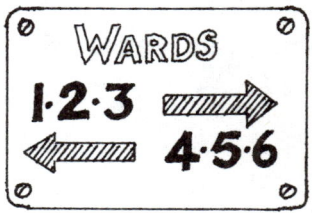

Is this simple?

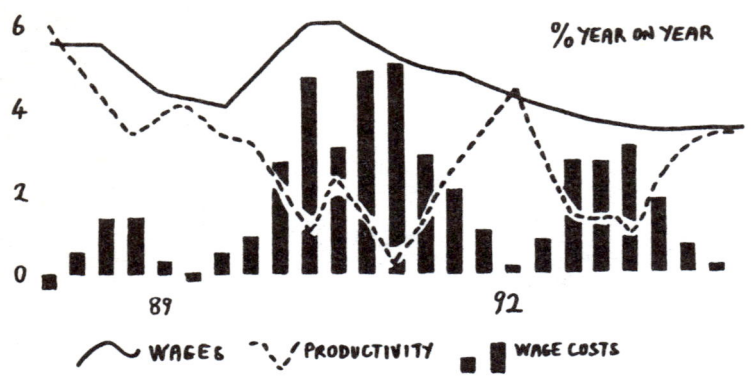

Is this legible, clear and simple?

> **What this means to you**
>
> Check that all your visuals are **legible**, **clear** and **simple**.

HOW TO MAKE A GOOD PICTURE

Stop saying 'I can't draw'

Look at this:

Of course it's the sun! Anybody anywhere in the world would recognize it instantly.

And most people in the world would know this is a windmill:

Here they are in context:

Pablo Picasso *Don Quixote* 1955 © DACS 1993

Can you find the donkey, too? Does anything strike you?

When you are drawing a donkey it is more important to make sure the ears are long than to waste time counting the legs!

> **What this means to you**
>
> We don't recommend you try to capture a complex human spirit, or the heat of midday, as Picasso could. But at the level of Sun, Windmill and Donkey you can draw pictures which will appeal in a direct and warm way to your listeners.

HOW TO MAKE YOUR PICTURE SUPPORT YOUR MESSAGE

Start with a clear message

It is very hard to draw a clear picture of a garbled idea.

Put another way: if your idea cannot be represented in a clear and simple picture, it is probably a woolly and undisciplined idea.

Or put yet another way: good, clear ideas translate easily into strong memorable images.

The acid test of many a management idea has occurred at the meeting entitled: 'How do we communicate this?'

Accept that it won't be easy

The professional propagandists and advertising experts charge high fees with good reason. It is very difficult to make a clear, memorable picture of your idea. But it is a skill which you can train.

Practice

Here's an exercise.

Make rough sketches to illustrate these ideas:

- Keeping fit can be terribly boring;
- Always telephone your mother on her birthday;
- A penny saved is a penny earned;
- Our department is overworked and short of resources;
- Our customers are eagerly awaiting the new product.

Use strong images only in support of your important points

If by now you appreciate the power of images to *reinforce* your central message, you will also accept a warning about the power of images to *undermine* the message, or *distract* the audience's attention.

The girly calendars so beloved of the motor spares trade are *objets d'art* in their own right. The motor mechanic who decorates his locker with Miss April, draped around a giant sparking plug, is not expected to make crucial purchasing decisions on that basis.

You should think twice before you project a colour photograph of your company's latest ergonomic work-station with a Miss April type perched on the corner of the desk. Most adult males in the audience will lodge the wrong thing in their memories. (Of course, if you think a picture of Miss April – or Mount Fujiyama, or the CEO – might put your audience in a receptive mood just *before* you display the work-station in all its glory, then that is a different decision.)

Similarly, if your priority statements One and Two are simply spoken, and unsupported by any visual appeal, it is a mistake to illustrate priority Three with a well-made graphic. It will loom disproportionately large in your audience's memories, over-shadowing the more significant items.

Be proud of the visual you have made

Something happens in our teens to make most adults very diffident about presenting anything faintly artistic. Karaoke bars depend on alcohol to help us overcome this inhibition.

If you have worked creatively, been thorough with your self-criticism, and tested your little masterpiece in rehearsal, it is wrong to be shy or apologetic. Say:

> I think this picture sums it up for me, and I invite you to consider it for a moment...

Or:

> There is one image I would like you to take away with you today, and here it is...

An illustrative anecdote.

A cocktail party was given at the offices of *New Yorker* magazine, and the Senior Editor met a cartoonist for the first time.

Editor: I looked closely at the last cartoon you did for us: there were only eight brush-strokes in it! And we paid you three thousand dollars...
Cartoonist: If I could have made the same joke with just seven brush-strokes, I would have charged you *five* thousand dollars.

What this means to you

Ask yourself:

> *In one short sentence, what do I want my audience to remember from this presentation?*

Then do everything you can to make a simple picture of that idea.

If you succeed, the clarity of the picture will feed back into the power of the words you choose, your confidence will grow, the picture itself will lodge in your audience's memory.

You will make much greater impact.

HOW TO HANDLE YOUR VISUAL AIDS

Trim the dead wood one last time

What do you sense when you are sitting in the audience and a presenter mounts the stage with both hands full of OHP slides? Pleasurable anticipation? A thrill of excitement, perhaps? Or a sinking feeling and an inward groan: 'Here comes another human stroboscope'?

When you are packing for a trip, it is natural to take a few things along 'just in case' – like handfuls of 'potentially useful' slides for your presentation.

When you arrive in your hotel room, take the 20 slides you packed for the trip, and spread them on the floor before you set off for the conference. Make three piles:

Need to show	Nice to show (Maybe)	No way
2	4	14

Take the first pile to the platform in your hand. Have the second in your briefcase: some of them might come in useful at the Question-and-Answer session. Bury the third pile under the dirty laundry in your holdall.

Make a final check of legibility and clarity

Many people check the switch of the OHP, some people check the focus.

Very few people ask a bystander to go to the back row and give an honest opinion of the key visual: 'I know this thing very well. Could you do me a favour and tell me what you see when I switch it on?'

Why not do it? Are you afraid you might hear an uncomfortable truth?

Avoid gadgetry

There are a lot of conference hotels and company training centres with:

- radio microphones (thump-clonk-hiss);
- laser pointers (tremble-wobble-jerk);
- remote control video consoles ('No, that's the Fast Forward, not the Pause'); or

- enthusiastic technical assistants who want to persuade you to try them.

Smile politely, and refuse.

A white board and/or a flip-chart, and a simple overhead projector, are all you will ever need.

Let your visuals speak...

...which is a polite way of saying,

Shut up while I'm looking at the nice picture

When you switch the OHP on, turn the page of the flip-chart, or unveil the scale model of the new yachting marina, step back and count 15 heartbeats before you speak.

It will seem like a very long time to you, but not to your audience.

What this means to you

You are in control – not the equipment, not the visuals.

Make your audience happy by letting them know they are in good hands.

Exercise:

You will need a watch with a second hand, and the business page from any newspaper.

Find a graph, look at your watch, and study the graph until you feel you have grasped its essential points.

Look at your watch.

If you were the audience at a presentation, that is how long it would take before you were ready for the presenter to start distracting you with his chatter.

THE INTERNATIONAL ARENA: PICTURES

We all adjust the way we explain a thing, or persuade a person, according to the age and experience of our listener. We speak differently to our accountants than to our teenage daughters.

Yet in the days of global business, it is very easy to stand before an audience of grey suits in an air-conditioned conference suite *and forget that they are from very different backgrounds.*

Don't worry too much

There *is* a set of behaviours proper to the international business community – the Frequent Flyers, the Hilton Culture.

It is fairly easy to Mind Your Manners in these circles, provided you behave in a gentle, moderate way. If your listeners are themselves members of the International Business culture, they will naturally forgive any minor gaffes you might accidentally perpetrate.

None the less, it is important to pay respect to the business card which your Japanese business partner gives you. At dinner in Switzerland, it is pleasant for everybody if you know how to handle your wine glass. And you will be more attractive as a business partner for a Muslim if you avoid unnecessary stress on deadlines and timetables.

Our message here is simple: 'if in doubt, ask somebody'.

So when using a visual to carry your message, make sure it means the same when it arrives at the receiver as when it left the transmitter.

Denotation (a fancy word for 'meaning')

Some cultures read from right to left, so the message advertising ACME indigestion pills doesn't travel very well:

Most English schoolchildren would be satisfied with these marks on their Arithmetic homework:

But in Sweden the meaning of ✓ and ✗ is reversed, so a visual saying:

  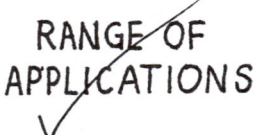

would deliver the wrong message.

What this means to you

Check your visual aid with a native of the culture you are addressing, asking:

Has this any meaning?

If so, what?

If something is wrong, work with a native to find an alternative visual which does deliver your message.
  If you cannot find one, do without any visual at all.

WHAT WILL STICK IN YOUR LISTENER'S MIND?/41

Connotations and associations (what it reminds you of)

The computer company's sales department produced a slide with a cartoon showing a lion-tamer, in the centre of the circus ring with his whip and revolver, and a number of well-disciplined lions disposed about the place. The idea was that the main computer program (lion-tamer) had the subsidiary routines (lions) well under control.

The visual was a disaster in a presentation to the civil service procurement department in a certain African country. For them, the lions were the spirit of the nation, subdued by a white man in the uniform of a colonial army.

In Western Europe or North America, if you draw a mouse badly, you can make it look more like a mouse by putting a piece of cheese in the picture – and you make the cheese look like cheese by drawing big holes in it.

In many parts of the world, cheese is soft runny stuff quite without holes. And mice have only been known to eat grain.

The piggy bank is a general symbol of money, savings and general prudence in the West. The convention is not recognized in countries where the pig is reviled as unclean.

Again we say: *check with a native.*

(There exist Dictionaries of Symbols covering all cultures, but usually they only define or explain the *denotations* of any symbol. So the Swastika, a very ancient symbol with great religious significance, might only have Nazism as the last entry on a chronological list of notes. The enormous *connotations* and *associations* of such symbols are often difficult to pin down academically.

A good way to tune in to the iconography of a culture you do not know well is to spend a little time watching the local TV commercials.)

3

What else will stick in your listener's mind?

STORIES AND EMOTIONS!

Visual stimulation without visual aids

To put a picture of Michael Jackson into the mind of your listener, you do not have to show him a picture.

You just have to *say* Michael Jackson, and he will immediately get a mental image of that great communicator. (Love him or hate him, you must admit that he knows his stuff.)

It will not be a complete picture. Perhaps just the lock of hair, the strange pallor, a dance-step. Perhaps one glittering glove.

It will be your listener's own picture. This is often more useful to you, as the presenter, than forcing your own picture upon him.

And in an audience of 50 people, you have created 50 personalized images – all enriched variations on your simple stimulus.

A famous 1960s radio advertisement went something like this:

Advertising on radio is primitive, you say? It has no visual impact? OK, one commercial coming up!

First, we empty Lake Superior...(Sound Effect of bath draining)

Next, we refill it with Chocolate Malted Milk . . .

And using every hose from the New York City Fire Department, we spray a fifty-foot layer of whipped cream on top...(Fire Engine Sound Effects)

And now, a five-ton maraschino cherry, dropped from a height of 30,000 feet. Cue the US Air Force...(Droning Big Bombers...SPLOSH!)

OK. Let's see you do that on TV!

> **What this means to you**
>
> Your listeners will paint themselves very rich personalized images if you tell them a simple story.

This is an unconscious but necessary process in the human brain; we would be quite unable to follow and understand the plot of an anecdote, a tale, or a saga without it. The pictures we make help us to follow the story step by step. Radio producers call it 'The Theatre of the Mind'.

This ability to visualize is precisely why stories are such a vigorous element in every human culture: we love to do the work of decorating a story in our minds.

You probably have stronger memories of stories you heard as a child, all those years ago, than you have of many recent presentations which had no story.

Stories are a vital tool in the memory of a tribe; they are used to pass on codes of ethics and a sense of tribal identity. The tales of Beowulf, King Arthur and The Thief of Baghdad were not originally made for the entertainment of children.

HOW TO TELL A USEFUL STORY

We define 'useful' here as meaning 'Helpful to your listener in remembering your important points'.

'How to Tell a Great Story', in the bar-room sense of 'Harry tells really great stories', is the subject of a quite different book. And different again if we are studying the craft of Herman Melville or Guy de Maupassant.

Even so, in a professional presentation we can borrow tricks from where we like...

Make your stories close to your listener's experience

If you are addressing an audience of trade unionists in the North of England, they will not warm to a story set in a gay New York disco.

Yet if you are speaking to an audience of young mothers, they will create vivid detail in their minds to support a story set in a maternity hospital.

Children will not really absorb tales of *crime passionel*, but farmers will empathize with stories about hard winters.

Shepherds, merchants, fishermen and soldiers in ancient Judaea wanted simple, memorable stories about people in their situation.

> **Borrow a technique from Christ's parables.**

Put people at the centre of your story

Even better, one central person.

Whole social systems have been illuminated by an author leading us through the adventures of one character – *Tom Jones, Candide,* Bazarov in *Fathers and Sons.*

So don't just say, 'There are difficulties for passengers transferring flights at busy airports in peak periods'. Say rather, 'There was a chap once travelling – or at least trying to travel – from Milan to Toronto via London Heathrow...'.

> **Borrow a tool from the novelists.**

Give names to your story-people

Cast your mind back to your childhood reading. How many names of characters can you remember? The list is surprisingly long. In some cases, you can remember the name more readily than the story – or you have the story filed in your mind under the name of the character.

What would the chocolate factory be without Willie Wonka? The story of Hansel and Gretel is absolutely their story. Long John Silver is not just an old sailor with a parrot and a wooden leg. He is LONG JOHN SILVER.

Don't just say, 'A colleague of mine the other week had an interesting adventure. He was travelling...'

Say instead, 'I have a colleague called John Doe. Some of you might have met him – big guy, fond of Guinness. Anyway, John Doe was travelling...'.

> **Borrow a trick from children's writers.**

Give your story a moral, and state it clearly at the end

Your story should have some point to it. Remember: just like a strong picture on the screen, the story will live in your audience's memory, so it should be connected with your message, shouldn't it?

We can reconstruct the message 'Slow and Steady Wins the Race', from the fable of The Hare and The Tortoise, by Aesop.

When we read La Fontaine's story of the fox, the crow and the cheese, we receive a warning about the Dangers of Vanity.

> **Borrow something from the fabulists.**

Let your audience do some of the work

'An Englishman, an Irishman and a Scotsman were waiting for the ferry...'. The bar-room story-teller does not tell us which tartan the Scotsman's kilt was made of. His listeners do not ask what time the ferry is due.

Leave out unnecessary detail and permit the imagination of each individual in your audience to supply one or two little dabs of colour.

> **Borrow from the bar-stool joke-teller.**

We have all had the experience of discomfort at a stage or screen adaptation of a story we already know: 'I don't think the dungeon scene was gloomy enough'; 'I've always seen Mr Pickwick as much fatter than that'; 'She's not at all my idea of a Fairy Godmother!'

Sometimes, it takes a clash between our imagination and the imagination of the director to make us realize that we had already painted our own pictures on the canvas of our minds.

> **What this means to you**
>
> Recognize the power of your listeners' imagination, and let it work for you.
>
> Be economical. Give the audience's minds a push in the right direction, and leave them to find their own conclusions.

> **The lazy uncle's way to tell a bedtime story**
>
> *Uncle*: OK, just one before you go to sleep. Now, shall we have a Mountain, a Forest, or a River?
> *Kid*: Forest!
> *Uncle*: Forest it is. Think about it for a moment, because I'll need you to describe it to me later.... Now, do we need a Witch, a Rabbit, or a Royal Canadian Mounted Policeman?
> *Kid*: Mountie!
> *Uncle*: What's his name?
> *Kid*: Wizwoz!
> *Uncle*: OK. Wizwoz the Mountie rode into the Forest.... What did you say it was like?
> *Kid*: All dark and wet and slimy with things in it.
> *Uncle*: We'll come back to the things later. First, we have to establish why Wizwoz was going into the dark, wet, slimy forest...
> *Kid*: Because that's where the dentist lived, and Wizwoz had toothache.
>
> *To be continued...*

So **visuals** are easy to remember, and **stories** are a good way to appeal to the visual part of the audience's mind. Anything else?

Yes. Sorry to say it, but your audience would love to see you displaying some **emotion**.

HOW TO CHANNEL THE POWER OF YOUR PERSONALITY

Be professional

Allow yourself to **feel** things: **think** sufficiently about that; then **do** something as a result. Nobody can ask more of you.

And for the purposes of this book, **do = speak**:

> There was no denying the fact that words spoken from a full heart carry more weight than all the artifices of rhetoric.
>
> C S Forester, *A Ship of the Line*

Displays of emotion are considered unprofessional in many environments – the bank manager's office, the doctor's surgery, the academic tutor's study. But wait!

How would you feel if your bank manager said: 'I've given a lot of thought to your case, and it would give me a great deal of pleasure to see you make the right decision. I sincerely believe...'.

Or the doctor: 'I've known you a long time now, and I really care for your welfare. I hate to see you damaging yourself with all this terrible rubbish you eat and drink...'.

Or the tutor: 'Let's stop mincing words, shall we? The reason you have been performing badly this year is that you are on the wrong course. It upsets me personally to say so, because as you know I love the subject, but...'.

Are these unprofessional statements? Only if they are insincere or backed by insufficient consideration. So decide if emotion is appropriate to the subject.

We see a spectrum:

INFORM ⎯⎯⎯⎯⎯⎯⎯⎯⎯⎯⎯⎯⎯⎯⎯⎯⎯⎯⎯ PERSUADE

Each presentation you make, or each section of each presentation, is positioned somewhere along this scale.

Towards the 'inform' end, when you are explaining how to read a gas meter, or the purpose of discounted cash flow forecasting, there is no place for passion.

The further you move towards 'persuade', the more you are free to show how strong your personal feelings are.

WHAT ELSE WILL STICK IN YOUR LISTENER'S MIND?/49

Exercise moderation

Hitler often appeared to lose control of his emotions. The power of his oratory sprang largely from this effect. Certainly his audiences perceived his rantings as totally sincere.

Trained actors are good at pretending to feel emotions. Yet Othello often smiles at the curtain-call, minutes after killing Desdemona and himself in an uncontrollable fit of jealous rage.

As a professional presenter, you should neither lose control, nor let the audience feel you are just putting on an act. But you *should* let your feelings show, in a direct and unaffected way, at crucial moments. The audience is very quick to read your feelings, and if the only feeling you have is boredom, they will see it and be infected by it. A little enthusiasm is very infectious.

Be true to yourself

We are pleased to welcome as our after-dinner speaker Sir Henry Trumpington, who has just returned from his epic trip by canoe and hang-glider from Alaska to Cape Horn. His presence among us is very fitting, I think. I have always felt very strongly that accountancy is an adventure.

This sort of thing makes an audience doubt the speaker's judgement, and even put him down as a bit of an idiot.

Only show emotions you really feel.

Practise the emotional moments

Will you transmit your happiness with a quiet smile, or by opening your arms wide and gazing heavenwards?

When you break the bad news, with furrowed brow, will your audience become depressed, or determined to work hard and improve things?

Can you talk about your own greatest hope for the future with controlled passion?

What this means to you

Your own convictions, your own atavistic powers as a communicator, the expressive range of your own facial muscles: these can be channelled by training, and positive results come very quickly.

THE INTERNATIONAL ARENA: STORIES

Re-select the telling details

We suggested earlier that you should only supply the evocative key ideas when you tell a story – leaving your listener's imagination to provide the rest.

When you are working across a culture gap you should take nothing for granted; ideas that conveyed themselves in oblique references at home might have to be spelled out more laboriously when you are playing away.

One of the present authors was asked to give a talk to a group of Hungarian managers from the textile industry: 'Total Quality Management and Customer Service'. He had the opportunity of a dry run with a couple of Hungarians in advance, and they gave him some advice.

The starting point had to be quite different. It could not be *assumed* that 'the customer is king'; the words had meaning, but would strike no personal chord with the audience – who had lived all their lives in a world where the supplier was king.

Similarly, ideas of 'Freedom of Choice', and 'Staff Involvement' had to be explained more fully than with a West European audience. And one key anecdote had to be scrapped. It began:

> You know what it's like when you're renting a car for the weekend, and your credit card has expired...

Very few Hungarians have ever rented a car. Fewer still hold credit cards.

Watch your language

This message is for you if you give presentations in English to non-native speakers, as is now so common in international business.

'Redundancy' is an important effect in language. Simply put, it means that an awful lot of what we say is unnecessary and repetitious. Often this is a good thing: if we build a lot of redundancy into our speech, we allow our listener to relax a little – he can follow the gist of what we are saying without concentrating on every single word.

Often, when we tell a well rehearsed anecdote, we use words much more economically, and try not to repeat ourselves. Often, the key idea in a story – like the punch-line in a joke – is expressed in very terse, Saxon language. Often, members of the audience who are more comfortable with Latinate formulations are left out in the cold.

The trick here is to select one or two of the audience who you suspect have less-than-perfect English. Watch them closely, particularly when you are warming up to an anecdote. When their eyes narrow or their shoulders tense, you should pause, and rephrase your last idea:

> ...and we certainly weren't going to let them get away with that!...we decided to make sure that it was impossible for them....

> ...but the decision was made, and there was no going back on it...it was quite irreversible....

> ...and we thought Paris to Nice in three hours was pretty good going...we were very satisfied with our progress....

You will often see a little smile of relief, or even a nod of gratitude. (This habit is quick and easy to develop, but only if you have eye contact with your audience. Make sure you have.)

Casual references that might not mean much when you're away from home

For the Swedish travelling abroad:
- ❑ Deep-snow driving techniques;
- ❑ Escaping from a hole in a frozen lake;
- ❑ Why bedroom curtains should be black.

For the British travelling abroad:
- ❑ Backing a horse;
- ❑ Supporting a football team;
- ❑ Buying health insurance.

For European city-dwellers travelling elsewhere:
- ❑ Feeding a parking meter;
- ❑ Arguing with a traffic warden;
- ❑ Playing golf with your bank manager;
- ❑ Discussing business with your wife;
- ❑ Getting drunk together as recreation.

The audience can lose the thread of what you're trying to say, while puzzling about such details.

THE INTERNATIONAL ARENA: EMOTION

Get your sincerity at the right pitch

When a Frenchman shrugs, and says 'Why not?', he is quite possibly giving whole-hearted endorsement to the proposal. In the same situation, a North German is more likely to *say*, 'I give my whole-hearted endorsement to the proposal'.

This is why the German stereotype of the French is 'Creative but feckless', while the French sometimes find the Prussians to be leaden, predictable and literal-minded.

Similarly, when an American speaks earnestly in praise of his company: 'We put our customer first at ABC, and we have the know-how to make fine products...', the Englishman on the adjacent bar-stool winces. It isn't really done to beat the drum that way.

Meanwhile, the American is probably wondering why the Brit persistently sells his company short: 'We do what we can and somehow we survive...'.

Your choice of words in the international arena is not so critical; between 'I'm keen on this project', 'I'm fond of this project' and 'I'm crazy about this project' the nuances fade.

More important are

1. *Facial expression*: Little to worry about here. Most facial expressions carry pretty universal meanings in the developed world. Most importantly, a cold and immobile face is likely to signal lack of enthusiasm almost everywhere. Be expressive but natural.

2. *Tone of voice*: English, well spoken from the platform, is one of the most expressive languages in terms of voice colour, pitch and tempo. (If you doubt this, listen to Swedish or Milanese Italian.)

3. *Body language*: There is plenty of specialist literature about regional differences in the meaning of hand and finger movements. Here we are only concerned with the projection of emotion.

    In Europe there is broad variation, generally along a spectrum from North to South. Finns stand still and perhaps get a tremble in the voice. Romans mobilize a rich vocabulary of gesture.

    If you are naturally demonstrative when you are on the

platform, that's fine. Remember to allow calm periods.

If you tend to be static and detached, do what you can to inject life at the moments of emotion. But be true to yourself. Aim for a contained, Michael Caine performance, rather than aiming for the histrionic high spots.

4

How can you draw your listeners into your story?

> I can listen for ages when someone is talking about me. After about two hours I begin to discern that the speaker is possessed of a great inner beauty....

You can buy clever audio cassettes for children these days, where the recording studio inserts the name of the recipient onto the tape:

> Cecily decided to escape while the giant was asleep, and tip-toed to the mouth of the cave. The giant opened one eye and roared, 'Where do you think you're going, Cecily?' (...and so on).

Cecily, of course, just can't get enough of this stuff. It has

> **You-appeal**

'Working' the audience

We assume now that you have captured your audience's attention (as in Chapter 1). They know the presentation is directed at them and they are prepared to listen and to trust you. Your job now is to hold their attention, and to help them to 'possess your idea'.

Most of this chapter is concerned with techniques of **persuasion**, well along the axis from the starting point of **information**.

Yet even when seduction is far from your mind – when your purpose is simply to deliver the data – your audience will respond much more positively if you remember to slant the information their way, giving it

> **'You'-orientation**

'YOU' IN INFORMATIVE PRESENTATIONS

When you set out to give a purely informative presentation, your audience presumably has a desire which matches: they want to gather information.

We have all suffered at the hands of the speaker who thought it was good enough simply to read out the text he originally wrote for publication in print. Perhaps he was lazy, perhaps he was nervous of making real contact with his audience, perhaps he was ignorant of a basic rule:

> **Written information should be easy to find**

> **Spoken information should be easy to remember**

Even university lecturers sometimes recognize, as examination time rolls round, that the students become more attentive if they say: 'You might bear this in mind during your Solid State Physics/18th-Century Literature paper next week...'.

When you are making a presentation, it is really just good manners to point out from time to time how your material is relevant to your listeners. More important, it is by pointing out the relevance that you help them lodge the data in their minds:

> Many of you would be here, half way up this axis...giving you a figure of 17 per cent if we read across to the curve...

or

> I've chosen an example of how our services operate in a big city setting, since I know most of you live in and around Milan...

or

> You're all doctors and scientists, and probably haven't concerned yourself much with financial matters – so far! But when they come to you in a few months and ask you to start taking budgetary responsibility, you'd be wise to concentrate on just a few key variables. For example...

Many speakers are afraid of overdoing this 'you' business; they think it seems forced or cheap. In fact, audiences have a very high tolerance for such direct appeals to their selfishness. Of course, it becomes laboured if you try to couch *everything* you say in terms of 'you and yours'.

HOW CAN YOU DRAW YOUR LISTENERS INTO YOUR STORY?/57

There are three times when the 'you' content should be high:
- ❑ at the beginning of your presentation;
- ❑ when you are delivering the central, most important points; and
- ❑ when you sense that you are in danger of losing contact with your listeners.

The first two should be dealt with at the preparation or writing stage; the third is a question of improvisation. A good speaker has a special mode of thinking, a kind of four-wheel drive, into which he can slip at a moment's notice. When he does, virtually everything he says is expressed in 'you' language, and he is gratified to see his listeners move forward half-an-inch in their seats.

Exercise

Express the following ideas so that the words 'you', 'your' and 'yours' appear as often as possible. The audience is a group of physical education teachers in their last week of training:

1. In all fitness training situations, the safety element is paramount.
2. When safety criteria have been met, it is time to consider the effectiveness of each training programme.
3. The personal attitude of the student is a crucial factor; training programme design should always take it into account.
4. For example, it is a mistake to set the student ambitious targets in the early days of training, if there is a danger that motivation might slip later. This is known as 'programming for failure'.
5. PE teachers succeed when they have the confidence of the students, individually and as a team. Setting achievable targets is the key to their confidence.

Of course we are here coming close to basic Sales Technique. The further you move along our **Inform** >>> **Persuade** axis, the more selling you are doing. And the more often you should:

> **Say 'you'**

'YOU' IN PERSUASIVE PRESENTATIONS

A tourist guide at the Tower of London, or a gunnery instructor in the Navy, has a pre-selected, ready-defined audience: these tourists want a little colourful history, a few family jokes, and time to take photographs; these sailors want to be technically perfect, and safe, and perhaps get promoted.

These are classic 'telling' situations. When it comes to 'selling' your idea, you have to do a lot more advance thinking about your audience:

> Who are they?

> Why are they here?

Find out who they are

Ask colleagues, secretaries, customers, suppliers, competitors, friends. Think hard and read up on their background culture, the commercial environment they work in, the character and habits of the key players.*

Get a clear picture of their sex, age, social class, education, functions, positions, expertise, experience, expectations, goals, fears, families, enemies, hobbies, tastes.

What are the relationships within the audience group? Are there any in-jokes? Who already knows the thrust of your argument, and who is ignorant? If you are hoping for a decision, how will it be made?

Once you have identified the decision-makers, it is even more important to find out what makes them tick:

> If you would work any man, you must either know his nature or fashions, and so lead him; or his ends, and so persuade him; or his weaknesses and disadvantages, and so awe him; or those that have an interest in him, and so govern him.
>
> *Francis Bacon, 1597*

---

* These aspects of preparation – for any presentation or negotiation – are dealt with thoroughly in *The New International Manager*, by Vincent Guy and John Mattock (Kogan Page, 1991).

HOW CAN YOU DRAW YOUR LISTENERS INTO YOUR STORY?

> **Exercise**
>
> Picture yourself manning a stand at The Boat Show. In the tank before you floats your company's latest product, a cabin cruiser with all sorts of features and gadgets, and a slightly souped-up version of your well-respected engine.
>
> Your sales literature is bland – a lot of photographs of the boat in nice locations, and tables of technical specs. No people.
>
> You have various systems for making payment 'easy', but long before you get to that stage you have to convince any prospect that this is *the* boat.
>
> Which of the boat's features will you emphasize as each customer agrees to climb aboard? How will you translate what is only a physical feature into a real, personal benefit for him?
>
> At 10.30, you are visited by a family – father, mother, boy of eight and girl of ten. At 11.15, a well dressed man in his middle twenties. Just after lunch, a retired gentleman.
>
> By afternoon tea, you might have sold separate cabins and a bit of privacy to the father, or safety equipment and peace of mind to the mother.
>
> The young man might have thought about the powerful engine note as a mating signal.
>
> The elderly gent, a fisherman perhaps, might have been lured by the copious storage space for his equipment and all the fish he dreams of catching.

Find out why they are here

Assume that your listener is coming to your presentation more or less voluntarily, and not just to kill time.

Ask yourself:

- ❑ What have I got that might satisfy his real need?
- ❑ What have I got that might tickle his appetite?
- ❑ What have I got that might enhance his self-esteem?

Need

If a man is hungry, tired, or cold, you do not have to make a presentation to persuade him to eat, sleep or sit by the fire.

The history of the Western world this century is littered with examples of goods and services that have moved from the realms of fantasy, through the world of luxury, into the category of necessity. (Cars, washing machines, holidays, insurance....)

Somewhere along the line, there has been some powerful persuading. A good recent example is the domestic smoke detector/fire alarm:

It makes a loud noise and helps you to sleep.

Appetite

Or, as some would have it, **greed** – for money, comfort, long life, pleasant sensations, beautiful things. All those matters you *could* get by without.

The big airlines know that 80 per cent of their revenue comes from 20 per cent of their clients – the regular business travellers. Watch how they try to attract these customers with wider seats, gorgeous flight attendants, a glass of champagne, special facilities at airports. (To avoid charges of sybaritism, a secondary message is sometimes appended: 'So that you can arrive refreshed and ready for serious decision-making'. An attempt to re-categorize **appetite** as **need**.)

Self-esteem

According to Maslow, this is where people will spend any resources they have left, once they are satisfied lower down the Hierarchy of Needs. However it expresses itself, the demand for good standing in the community is a powerful one.

Keeping Up With The Joneses has been recognized as a social force since the 1950s – although for a tiny minority of the population, display and ostentation have always been important.

Of course, no sane person will be attracted by a status symbol before his basic needs are satisfied. And they can quickly cast away status symbols when they are under direct physical threat:

A horse! A horse! My Kingdom for a horse!

There is often a blurring of distinctions between **appetite** and **self-esteem**. Some people will deny themselves tangible comforts, in order to buy a socially acceptable outward appearance.

To return to our airline example: everybody knows, though few officially admit, that the extra cost of a Business Class ticket has much more to do with one-upmanship than with extra efficiency or better food – 'The most expensive after-dinner mint you will ever eat'.

As fashions shift, conspicuous consumption becomes more or less acceptable. Advertisements from more blatant periods seem crass in less overtly materialistic times: 'For the few who can afford it...'.

> **What this means to you**
>
> The more you find out about your audience, the more chance you stand of triggering a response when you make your presentation.
>
> You should ask yourself if your 'offer' will appeal to them at the level of **need**, **appetite**, or **self-esteem**.
>
> Large corporations invest in Market Research to identify emerging demands in the population. Then they adapt their product range and promotion – the offer – to suit. On a personal scale, you should follow the same procedure. Then,
>
> ❑ If they really *need* what you are offering, and you have no competition, just to explain it clearly will be enough.
>
> ❑ If you are trying to tempt their *appetite*, with an attractive but unnecessary treat, organize your argument accordingly.
>
> ❑ If your proposal has no concrete advantage, but will boost their *self-esteem*, it might be necessary to dress it up as something more substantial. Find a way to suggest they really *need* it.

So far in this chapter we have assumed that the audience is more or less interested in the facts you have to give them. Further, we have supposed that at some level they are directly sympathetic to the proposal you have to make.

We are often asked 'How can I overcome resistance, even hostility, in my audience?'

There is a problem with that question: the use of the word 'overcome'. It suggests a frontal attack in force. As a presenter, you do not want to invade your audience's territory, you want to settle it.

CONFLICT OR CONFLUENCE?

Think of your message as a vector

Let us suppose you have an idea to put forward – idea *x*. You want to affect your listener by expressing *x* – change his attitude, sway him, bring him round to your way of seeing things. In any language, metaphors for persuasion involve *moving* the listener, or changing the direction of his thought.

So *x*, we can say, has a direction:

X also has force. The power of the idea is affected by two things: the strength of your commitment to it, and the devices you use to implant it in your listener's mind – emotion, plus your tool-kit of techniques.

Let us suppose that you feel quite strongly about *x*, and express the idea fairly forcefully.

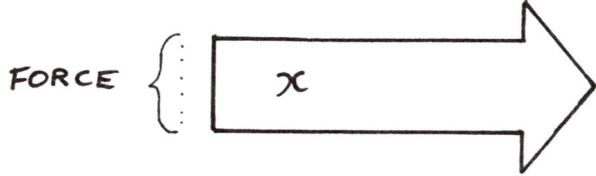

So an idea becomes a message.

Will the message change your listener's position? That depends very much on his initial attitude.

If he is somehow against idea *x*, and his arguments – rational or emotional – are as strong as message *x*, there will be a stand-off.

So if your listener has attitude *y*:

then

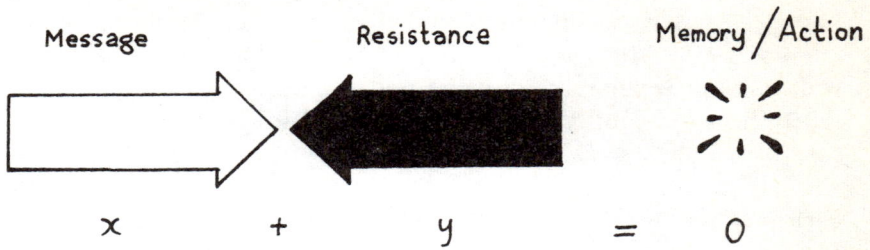

Your listener will reject your message; he will fail to remember it, or fail to act on it.
Here are two examples of this:
x: You really must try this lobster bisque, it's delicious!
y: I'm allergic to seafood, in any form.

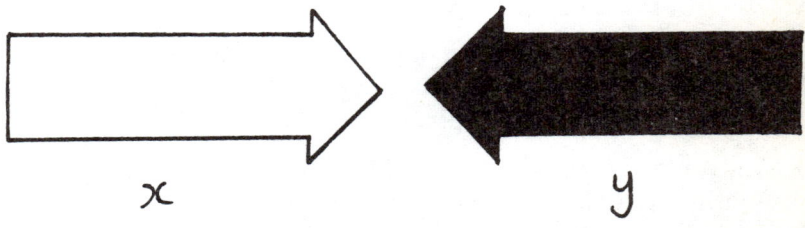

or

x: This product is nearing the end of its life cycle, and I believe we should stop promoting it – or indeed withdraw it completely.
y: In some of our regional subsidiaries, this product represents about half their sales turnover.

In the case of the lobster bisque, the **no sale** signal is loud and clear. A similar thing happened when Galileo tried to persuade the *curia* that the earth was in orbit around the sun.

If there is a strong factual or dogmatic block, you can save your breath, or change your objectives. The speeches of politicians are designed to change not the opinions of the people they attack, but the opinions of those who are listening.

In the less dramatic case of the product that needs to be dropped, it is clear that the listener will take no positive action. In fact, he will probably forget that the idea was ever put forward.

This is one of the hardest lessons for any presenter to learn: your listener is very strongly inclined to ignore or forget what you say to him, especially if what you say to him tends to upset his carefully balanced view of the world.

Add a little passion – in small doses

What happens if you repeat and reinforce your argument? A bit of patience and a bit of passion....

What happens if message x is presented more forcefully? If, after an initial rejection, a little crude enthusiasm is injected:

> x: What about Spain this year?
> y: Not keen. I don't speak a word of Spanish, and I like to be able to get by in shops and restaurants.
> x: Ah, Spain! That's the place to go this year! Viva España! Olé! (She puts a rose between her teeth and stamps her feet.)
> y: OK, OK. Phone up for some brochures, if you like.

Here we are talking about a *campaign* of persuasion, not a single presentation.

Back to our business example, a few days later:

> x: This product is finished! Dead! If we spend any more money promoting it, we'll be pouring it down the drain. We must cut our losses now and scrap the bloody thing!
> y: In some of our regional subsidiaries, this product represents almost half their sales turnover. Still, if you feel that strongly about it, I suppose I could sound them out – gauge their reactions.

In this case, y has at least recognized and lodged x's feelings about the contentious product. But 'I suppose I could investigate' is not exactly 'I agree. Let's scrap it!'

HOW CAN YOU DRAW YOUR LISTENERS INTO YOUR STORY?

Match your vector to your listener's

You might be very lucky. The antipathy to your idea might suddenly melt away. Your listener might say: 'At last! Somebody's come out and said it!'; 'You must have read my mind!'; 'I couldn't have put it better myself!'.

In such cases, the message x delivers will not only be well remembered, and even acted upon – it will be magnified... augmented...multiplied.

x: I think it's quite important.
y: I think it's quite important, too.

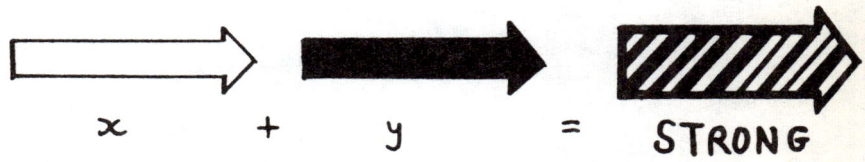

Picture an old-fashioned child's bowling hoop rolling towards you:

Now you deliver a stroke to the top of the hoop, just enough to stop it dead:

Or rather more than that – give it a well-timed whack, and it might stumble off in the reverse direction:

Now picture the hoop coming up from behind – moving your way already:

Help it on its way:

And it moves faster:

Of course, the right way to build up the hoop's speed and maintain its momentum is to run along beside it, giving it a gentle push from time to time – far more effective than one almighty shove at the beginning.

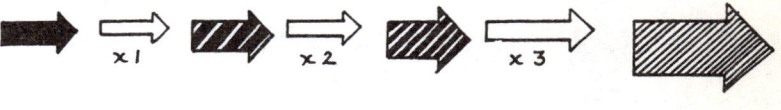

Find a vector that's going your way

For a start, don't try to push seafood on somebody who is allergic. Anybody who has ever suffered an allergic attack after a lobster dinner will remain strongly averse forever:

But let us consider the other two cases – the Spanish holiday and the product deletion.

Here the listener's attitudes were less monolithic. They were a complex of thoughts and emotions – strong and weak, in favour of the speaker's idea and against it, directly and tangentially:

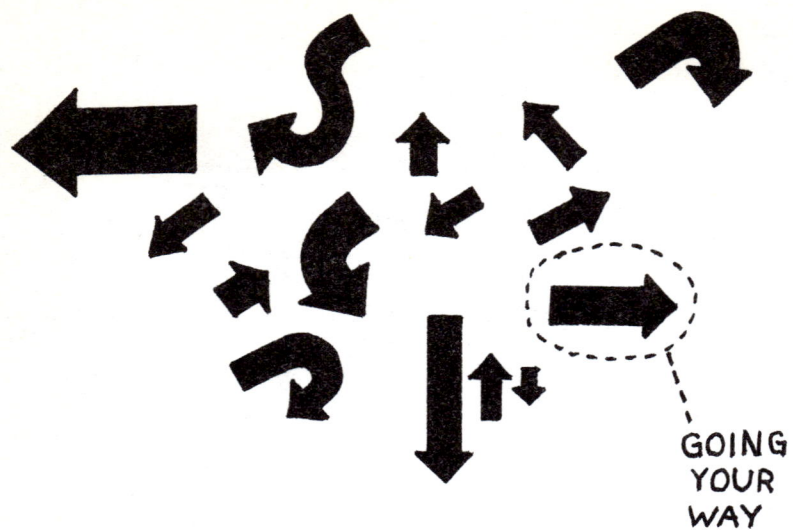

Do it carefully...

Teenagers sometimes discover this trick:

> *Daughter*: Dad, you know you're always saying we spend too much on bus-fares...
>
> *Father*: No, you can't have a motor-bike!

It takes experience to handle the technique with subtlety.

...perhaps even openly

Persuasion is not necessarily a dark art or a dirty trick.

If you have established yourself as a trustworthy person in the first minutes of your presentation, why risk being caught out as a trickster now?

There is a great force in signpost-statements like:

> I've thought a lot about your situation, and I think I can convince you .... (By the way, 'convince' sounds less dangerous and slippery than 'persuade'.)

or

> There is one factor in your life which means you should consider my proposal seriously...

HOW CAN YOU DRAW YOUR LISTENERS INTO YOUR STORY?

or

Clearly you will have several arguments against my idea, but let's consider the aspects you approve of....

What this means to you

If you want to *persuade* your listener, you should find that vector in his make-up which most closely coincides with your own purposes.

Then give it a gentle series of nudges – during a single presentation if you must, over a series if you can.

At every stage, use all your other skills as a presenter to give your strategy the best possible chance of working.

Finally, try a little honesty.

THE INTERNATIONAL ARENA

'You'

If you are facing a mixed nationality group, it helps if you can provide selected examples to bring your material home to them:

> So this is where the *Independent* fits in the socio-political mix. For comparison, I've marked positions here for *Le Monde* and *Frankfurter Allgemeine Zeitung*.

(If an Italian then asks for help, and you know nothing of the Italian press, somebody else in the audience will probably come to your help. Then you have a discussion. Wonderful.)

Need, Appetite, Self-esteem

Your message will require careful modification as you move away from home base – and not just to the way it is phrased.

An audience in Atlanta might respond very positively if you appeal to their sense of privilege – 'you deserve the most expensive, and everyone knows this is it'.

The same message would go down badly in Scandinavia, where it is eccentric, and even wicked, to flaunt one's wealth.

Persuasion: conflict or confluence?

Similarly, different cultures have different ideas on manipulation and bullying. (We will stay with Scandinavia and the USA.)

It has been observed, for example, that many Swedes lack 'the killer instinct' in business – that they are all naïve, blue-eyed honesty. They have been conditioned by their culture and now view 'persuasion with a dash of psychology' as 'shameful dirty tricks'.

If a Swedish audience suspects that you are attempting insidious manipulation, they will quickly turn against you and switch their minds off.

On the other hand, there remains a dash of 'Michael-Douglas-In-Wall-Street' in the American way of business. In the USA, they just might respect you if they think you are a shrewd and determined dealer.

HOW CAN YOU DRAW YOUR LISTENERS INTO YOUR STORY?/71

What this means to you

Do your homework. Learn as much as you can, in pleasurable ways, about your listener's culture.

Build a flexible model of that culture, and use it to interpret the things you hear, and adapt the things you say.

Don't be nervous of *using* what you know.

5

Can you really change your listener's beliefs?

So you have established your credentials, employed well-chosen devices to attract your audience's attention and lodged your idea in their memories, and laced the whole thing with lots of you-appeal.

Now the deeper question:

> **Can you really change your listeners' beliefs?**

We left Mark Antony at the end of Chapter 1, convincing the plebs that he was just like them, really.

He has earlier stated, in soliloquy, his objective in this oration: 'Woe to the hand that shed this costly blood!' – the turncoat assassin, Brutus, must pay the price. The means is to be 'Domestic fury and fierce civil strife', and Mark Antony has decided that the Roman mob should get things rolling.

People remember the speech for the way he handles his message to the mob – 'Caesar was *not* an ambitious tyrant. He loved you and you should avenge him'.

He drips the idea into them gradually, letting them work things out for themselves – but always with his guidance. Then, when he starts to give them his message directly, they recognize it as something they already 'know'. And now here is this excellent fellow telling them that he believes it, too. It must be true.

(By the way, history shows us that large audiences can be easier to sway than small, critical groups. In large numbers, people tend to feel, think and act uniformly. Shakespeare learned this from the classical authors, and from observation.)

At the **persuasion** end of the spectrum, *you are trying to manage people's beliefs*. If we accept that as a general objective, then the challenge is

> **To make your message serve your objective,**

and

> **to handle your message effectively.**

Keep your objective clearly in mind

When you are making your presentation, there are many temptations:

- ❑ to stay on safe ground; to try something new and daring;
- ❑ to fill the time available; to make it nice and short so we can have a long lunch;
- ❑ to exaggerate small matters for dramatic effect; to understate important points because they seem so obvious.

These activities all have their place, *provided they are serving your objective*.

Everything that carries you in the right direction offers a good setting for your message. (We are supposing that you have set yourself a *reasonable* objective. If your goal is ambitious, consider the model of the bowling hoop we offered earlier: gentle nudges over a period of time are the best way to change a person's way of thinking.)

What this means to you

At the planning and design stage of your presentation, you should return again and again to the question:

Will this help to get me where I want to be?

Let your message work for itself

When Lego, the children's building toy, was first introduced, the starter pack was a big box with all sizes and colours of bricks, plus a few doors and windows. Supplementary packs could then be bought: more specialized bricks, garage doors and so on. They were priced to be just about right for an aunt to buy for Little Willie's birthday.

Some years later, Lego changed the nature of the supplementary packs. Each one could now be used to only one purpose: to make a helicopter, or to make a telephone box....

Sales among aunties rocketed. They had never really liked the previous arrangement, because Little Willie used to mix the bricks from Aunty's birthday present in with all the others, and lose some under the sofa. Now she could buy him a nice helicopter to assemble and put on the shelf where she could see it on her next visit. The advertising and point-of-sale material left the message unspoken. It was better for Aunty to work it out for herself.

We are often asked on training seminars: 'Should I tell my audience at the start what it is I hope to convince them of?'

We say yes, if it seems appropriate. The Lego company was quite open about wanting people to buy the product. But usually it is better not to over-explain the message.

An audience that has arrived at its own conclusions is more thoroughly convinced of those ideas – 'their own' ideas – even if you have helped them to germinate.

What this means to you

Distinguish between your objective and your message. Your objective can be stated clearly; your message is what moves your audience towards it.

Decide which parts of your message the audience could work out for itself. Then give them the information they need to start them thinking.

Make your audience reach out for your idea

Antony: ...But here's a parchment, with the seal of Caesar... Which, pardon me, I do not mean to read...

Shakespeare, Julius Caesar, III (ii)

The mob, of course, is soon screaming for Mark Antony to read Caesar's last will out to them.

With more subtle audiences, these pantomime tactics might not work. But is it really such a different ploy when the speaker says:

I've studied the situation long and hard, and I've got a few novel ideas, but I don't think I should push them at you...,

or

There's one other piece of evidence which, for me, is a clincher – but most of you have probably already guessed...,

or

> **What this means to you**
>
> Don't just *give* your ideas to the audience.
>   Set a puzzle for them, let them work on it, suggest you have an answer, let them ask for it.
>   Dig a hole, push them in, offer to help them out. They can't refuse.
>   This is the right moment for a little flattery – 'There you are, you see! You got out of the hole.'

Now that clearly raises an important question, but it wouldn't be fair for me to preempt your judgement...?

Convert your key points into rhetorical questions

In the first half of Mark Antony's big scene, he says:

> Did this in Caesar seem ambitious?
>
> Was this ambition?
>
> What withholds you then to mourn for him?
>
> Will you be patient? Will you stay awhile?
>
> You will compel me then to read the will?
>
> Shall I descend? And will you give me leave?
>
> Kind souls, what weep you, when you but behold
> Our Caesar's vesture wounded?

Pointing Caesar's bloodied, tattered toga out to them, and *still* not having read out the will, Mark Antony offers:

> Good friends, sweet friends, let me not stir you up
> To such a sudden flood of mutiny.

(The first time mutiny has been mentioned, incidentally.)
  Rhetorical questions are very powerful, and equally risky. Everybody is embarrassed when they go wrong.

  Orator: Are we mice, or men?

  Audience: Squeak!

or

CAN YOU REALLY CHANGE YOUR LISTENER'S BELIEFS?

Orator: Have you ever dreamed of owning your own cabin cruiser?

Audience: Not really, no. Can't say I have.

or

Orator: When was the last time you really felt financially secure?

Audience: Last month when I got my pay-cheque.

But correctly used, they draw your audience in:

Now, how many of our big customers - Category A here – do you suppose were down in Category D five years ago?

Is there any reason not to start thinking about the long-term future now?

Why not set resources aside for this project, while we have spare resources to hand?

What this means to you

Did you read the title of this section?
Is a direct statement the only way of making a point?

Exercise

Convert these statements into rhetorical questions. (Your audience is a group of German, American and French Human Resource specialists. They all work for companies which have recently embarked on Joint ventures with East European Companies.)

- ❏ It will not be easy to graft Western management styles onto local working practices.
- ❏ Local managers will feel resentful...especially if you are planning 40 per cent staff cuts.
- ❏ Western Organisation Development consultants know little about the cultures of these areas.
- ❏ You should consider, as a first step, employing local management psychologists to advise you.

Sh! (or: *The pause that refreshes*)

- Don't put one question inside another, like Russian dolls:

    Orator: I ask you: Is the time ripe for a new policy? But do we have the right men to implement it? Where are we to find such men?

    Audience: Er...yes, no, and ... what was the last question?

- Pause for a long time, quite still, after each individual question.
- Resist the temptation to answer the question yourself.
- Watch the body language; you can often read the moment when they have found the answer within themselves. They nod, or blink, or change position in their seats.

What this means to you

When you have asked a question, give your audience time to think about the answer.

You needn't wait for them to speak the answer, often you can say:

I hope that has set you thinking. Now let's move on to our next point...

Build up your audience's confidence in you

Spending all this time on the edge of their seats, your audience need to know that they are in good hands.

Their confidence in you is based on your personal credibility – your honesty, your altruism, and your consistency. It is also dependent on what they perceive as your competence – your command of the subject, and your power to make things happen.

We return to the question of competence in a later section, which is devoted to Question-and-Answer sessions; it is in Question-and-Answer sessions that your competence is probed.

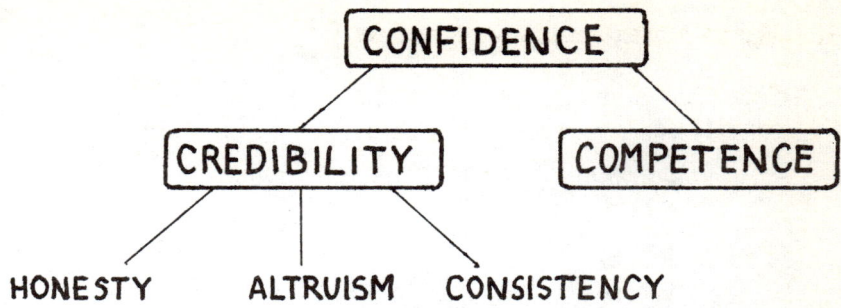

Maintain your credibility

Personal credibility is of course vital for politicians, and it is hard for them to maintain in a world of electioneering up and downs, media distortion, and promises broken for *raison d'état*.

They ring the changes on honesty, altruism and consistency. If, at a given moment, they appear weak in one of these virtues, they make a lot of noise about one of the others:

I confess I lied last time (0/10 for honesty).
I did it to help poor people (10/10 for altruism).

I confess I lied last time (0/10 for honesty).
I was so bound up in pursuit of my single, overriding objective (10/10 for consistency).

I drew personal benefit from that strategy (0/10 for altruism).
I have openly published all the details (10/10 for honesty).

I drew personal benefit from that strategy (0/10 for altruism).
I could not let fear of criticism sway me from what I held to be the best course of action (10/10 for consistency).

I have changed my mind (0/10 for consistency).
I have new information which compels me to do so (10/10 for honesty).

I have changed my mind (0/10 for consistency).
I fight on for the same underlying cause (10/10 for altruism).

Next time you watch a senior politician on the spot, look out for this technique.

> **What this means to you**
>
> To maintain the audience's confidence in you, you should strive always to be:
>
> ❑ Honest, truthful, accurate, and respectful of facts.
>
> ❑ Altruistic – or at least disinterested, generous, and constructive.
>
> ❑ Consistent, reliable and thorough.
>
> If you manage most of this most of the time, you will be seen as a healthy source of good ideas that can safely be imbibed.

Distil your message

The expression 'Central Message' describes that point in a presentation when you deliver, in a few well-chosen words, the one idea you want your audience to take away with them.

Most people remember the ironical drumbeat in Mark Antony's oration:

> For Brutus is an honourable man,
> So are they all; all honourable men...
>
> But Brutus says he was ambitious,
> and Brutus is an honourable man... (repeated three times)

Yet Brutus' fate is sealed when Mark Antony singles him out as the vilest of all the conspirators. By agreement, they all stabbed Caesar, but Brutus was Caesar's favourite:

> This was the most unkindest cut of all.

HOW TO MAKE A GOOD CENTRAL MESSAGE

❑ Use Saxon, not Latin vocabulary: 'Blood, toil, tears and sweat' is better than 'Blood, labour, tears and sweat', and much better than 'blood, labour, tears and perspiration'.

❑ Employ active, not passive constructions: don't say 'This contract will be won by our sales force'; say 'Our sales force will win this contract'.

- ❏ Set up contrasts: 'It isn't cheap, but it'll save you money in the long run.' ('I come to bury Caesar, not to praise him'.)
- ❏ Use terms close to your listeners: ('If some guy's got a dollar he didn't work for, some guy's worked for a dollar he didn't get.' (Marx's *Capital* in one sentence.)

THE INTERNATIONAL ARENA

Every civilization has surely had its own style of rhetoric, and its own rules of debate. Yet Hollywood has enjoyed making everyone from Moses to Davy Crockett speak in the same voice, strike the same chords in their audiences' minds and hearts. And Hollywood has got away with it.

This is because cinema audiences recognize certain universals:

- ❑ In all times and in all places, audiences have reacted to a well-shaped, well-delivered message in the same way.
- ❑ In all times and in all places, clever speakers have designed and transmitted their messages according to the same basic principles.

Evoke, don't dictate

The first messages of this chapter:

> **Keep your objective in mind**
>
> **Let your message work for itself**
>
> **Make your audience reach out for your idea**
>
> **Use rhetorical questions**
>
> **Sh!**

all hold true wherever in the world you might be speaking.

Audiences from the old communist world are used to being harangued and hectored into a set of prescribed beliefs. Audiences of Americans who failed to go on after High School are used to being given answers without first being provoked into thought.

In either case, they might be puzzled for a moment when you allow them to range freely in search of their own conclusions. However, they will soon take to it – and remember you very clearly as the speaker who handled his message in a new and better way.

What this means to you

Stick to the same rhetorical devices when you work across a culture gap. Allow your audience time for adjustment if they seem to need it.

Choose the right man for the job

On the question of **confidence and credibility**, it must be said that deep cultural programming exists.

It will be very difficult for an audience of senior Japanese executives to take seriously proposals made by a boy of 25.

An audience of Iranian men will find it hard to listen seriously to a woman with long blond hair.

Watch your language

Our point about the power of Saxon words ('killing' and 'eating', rather than 'assassination' and 'nourishment') is true in Northern Europe, and generally in the USA.

If you are delivering your message where Romance languages are current, Latin-based terms are easier for an audience to process. 'We didn't sell as many as we'd expected to, dammit!' should be 'translated' into 'Unfortunately, we failed to achieve our objective with regard to sales'.

6

How should you build and deliver your argument?

STRUCTURE AND PACING

You have thought about your audience – particularly:

❑ their level of knowledge (in the case of an informative presentation); or

❑ their needs and appetites (in the case of a more persuasive performance).

You have selected very stringently from the information available; pared the ideas down to an effective minimum.

The question now is how to impose some **structure** on the material.

For the sake of structure in this section, we will move along our spectrum from **inform** to **persuade**, pausing about half-way along in an area we will call **teach**, to see what we can learn from speakers in university lecture halls and high school classrooms.

Go from general to particular

In a purely *informative* presentation, your starting point is determined by the level of knowledge of your audience. How much do they already know? OK, we'll start from there.

If you are addressing a split-level audience, including experts, amateurs and ignorami, you have a problem. Go for the middle, perhaps saying:

> Many of you already know this, but please be patient while I set the scene....

Then *set the scene*. Give them the general context, the broad background. Put them in the picture. Then say:

> Within this context, I'd like to *focus* now on one particular item....

Then deliver the goods.
At this point it is right to say,

> I will be concentrating on *the most striking aspects*, but there will be more information handed out at the end.

Give the audience a *Route Map*:

> I'll be talking for about 15 minutes, leaving time for questions at the end. By then, we should have covered three main points – x, y and z.

And plant *signposts* along the way:

> So that covers x. If there are no immediate questions I'll move on to y...

> And that's all we have time for on the subject of y, so turning our attention to z....

When you have finished with the specifics, say,

> Now let's remind ourselves of how this fits in *the overall picture*...

Then give a broad-brush *summary*. It will help your audience commit the whole thing to memory.

Your job is to inform, and help the audience remember; you are not a stand-up comic. Your audience has limited powers of concentration, and you owe it to them to make sure that they know where they are every step of the way.

When you lay out a written report, you make full use of *chapter titles*, *headings*, and *paragraph* breaks, so that your reader can find his way around the text – and find his place again if he puts it down for a while.

Life is tougher for your listener at a presentation. He can't run his eye back up the page to see where he got lost; you don't come equipped with a rewind button. Give him all the help you can.

Measure their interest

In the 15th century, knowledge was a rare, precious and fascinating commodity. People survived in a dearth of news and information about the wide world. When a speaker came with fresh data – a visitor to the village, a soldier returned from the war, a monk from a distant abbey – they were rapt.

The same level of attention might be found today when an

internationally famous professor speaks to a tickets-only audience on a special occasion. Otherwise, however, audiences in the industrialized world are swamped with information. They overdosed long before you took the platform. They don't really want you to give them too much more.

What this means to you

Decide how important and interesting your information really is for your audience. Be honest....

If you can truly say that they are enthusiastic about what you can deliver, then fine. Just let them have it. On the other hand, you might come to realize that what you have to offer is only moderately enticing.

In such cases, you should spend a few minutes at the start – in a separate, persuasive presentation – convincing them that the material you have is vital to them.

Either way, the information should then be transmitted in a well organized, clearly labelled package.

Select the information to suit your audience's world

One of the present authors was involved with a company which had taken on a large group of immigrant guest workers, and housed them in guest accommodation blocks (or 'barrack-sheds', as the workers insisted on calling them).

A senior manager addressed them early in their stay, with a motivational message about the company's plans for growth, and the important part they had to play in those plans. He left it to a junior to give them the workaday stuff, like:

- ❑ where to complain about the food in the canteen;
- ❑ where to complain about the toilet facilities; and
- ❑ the rules about women visitors in the barracks.

Months later, after experiencing interventions from various executives, they still remembered the junior's presentation, and referred to him as 'the only clever man in the company'.

Even when your information is well organized and relevant, there will be times when your audience needs perking up a bit.

Start with a bang

It is rather dreary to begin with: 'This all began in 1873...', or 'Quite a lot of people have installed equipment like this without much difficulty...'.

Speak in the present, or even better the future, at the start of your presentation. Tempt the appetite with one specific, telling detail.

> Next week sees the culmination of 120 years of development....., or

> My next-door neighbour is using this equipment now, and it only took him a weekend to install it.

A good press release follows these rules, as does the newspaper story which is based on the release. The Press Relations specialist writes the press release, and the lazy page editor just uses the first two paragraphs, or the first six inches, or whatever.

Both professionals share an aim: to grab the reader's attention.

> **Borrow a technique from the Press Relations specialist.**

Make contact early

Let your audience know from the start that you intend to interact with them: 'Old Harry there was telling me in the bar earlier...'

> **Borrow from the night club compere.**

Use the high spots on the concentration curve

The concentration/retention span of an audience looks like this:

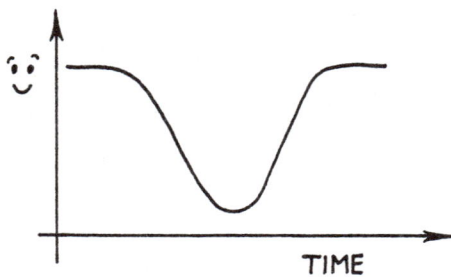

People absorb and retain the things they hear first and the things they hear last. They doze off in the middle. This is true of any speech lasting longer than five minutes.

The good teacher knows about the concentration/attention curve, and takes it into account. He gives his class the most useful information at the beginning of the lesson, and at the end.

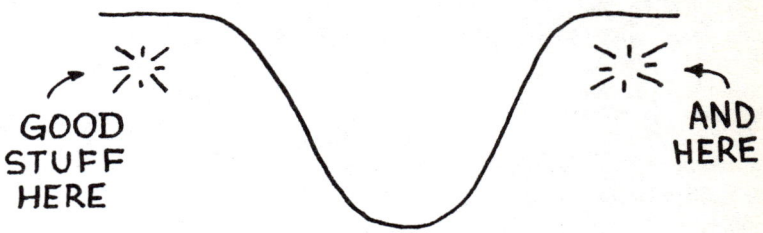

Of course, it would be nice to create a few more peaks of attention:

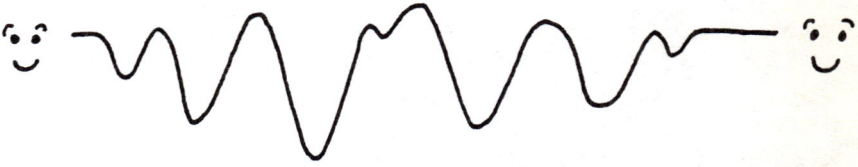

How can you do that?

This is where we deviate from discussion of structure itself, to the issue of **pacing** – upping or cooling the tempo.

Use your voice

Keep it up. A series of falling cadences sends people to sleep. A mumbling delivery makes you seem unsure of yourself, and undermines their confidence in your message.

At key moments, turn up the amplitude and the frequency, the dB and the Hz, the volume and the pitch. And remember all we said in the last chapter about the importance of pauses.

> **Exercise**
>
> It is possible to create effects using nothing more than carefully judged silences.
>
> In the appendices is a text of the Gettysburg Address. With your pencil, mark pauses on it (with a //). Then read it aloud in a flat, undramatic voice. See how much energy, tension and emotion you can inject just by stretching the pauses out.

Change your equipment

Move from OHP to flip-chart and back again. Use the white board. The variety of stimulus helps your audience stay alert. (We have already said our piece about laser pointers and such temptations: avoid them.)

Change the way you look

If you are good at histrionic gestures, we don't aim to teach you anything from the pages of a book. We are not talking about the ability to cry at will, or get under the skin of a character from Chekhov, but the knack of shifting register, from formal to relaxed, from static to demonstrative.

If you're not a natural in this department, and you don't want to go to drama classes, you can:

- *Change your position on the stage*, moving left to right, front to back, coming out from behind the lectern;
- *Take some notes out of your pocket*, like Harold Macmillan, who used to fumble for a (blank) sheet of paper and 'refer to it' – just to build up the tension;
- *Take your glasses off*, or screw your monocle in;
- *Sit down; stand up.*

Make them do something

Circumstances rarely permit you to have your audience rolling round on the floor or swinging from the rafters. But for the sake of involvement, you should explore the limits of your setting. Get them to: clap hands; hold hands; empty their pockets; write an answer on a scrap of paper ('OK, now hands up everybody who guessed more than 35 per cent'); close their eyes for a moment: stand up/sit down.

Tell a joke

We mean a 'joke' joke – the story with a punch-line. But only tell them if you really are a good teller of jokes, and if the joke in some way serves your objective.

When you next tell a joke at a party, and the people laugh, look around you: are they *really* amused, or just being polite? Unless you are above-average-funny, leave jokes out of your presentation. They will be painful. The awfulness is compounded if a senior manager, who is bad at telling jokes, insists on telling them from the presentation platform. The sycophantic laughter of his subordinates is a very ugly sound.

Remember that less is more

Be economical with your effects.

Refer back to chapter 2

...where we deal at length with the power of visuals, stories and emotions.

Colour-and-Movement, the child psychologists call it. It will snap your audience out of their revery, and bring them back where they belong – attending to your message.

What this means to you

Like the best teachers, you can manufacture a series of attention-peaks in your presentation, by stimulating your audience's senses.

The most powerful *structure* for a presentation is best suited to the *persuasion* game. It naturally brings your audience to the point where they agree with you, your objective, and the means to that end.

We make *everyday decisions* like this:

> Today I'm going to a meeting with a client. So it has to be the dark blue suit. Which shirt shall I wear?
>
> I like the pale grey, but it's in the wash....Or I could wear the pink stripe, but I haven't got a tie to go with it...or...or...

Fine, I'll wear the white one with the button-down collar.

> **Exercise**
>
> Think about other small decisions you have made recently within the same structure - your journey to work, perhaps, or what to give your guests for dinner.

In *problem-solving conversations*, we say:

> The kids are growing up now, and we're going to need an additional bedroom soon...
>
> I suppose you could give up your study, and do your writing in the kitchen...
>
> I don't fancy that... what about you working some overtime, so we could afford a bigger flat?
>
> Or...
>
> Or...
>
> Good, then that's agreed. We look around the cheaper areas of town, to see if we can find a house with a bit more space for the same money.

In the nature of things, and especially when resources are limited, the resolution is usually a compromise.

In *persuasive presentation*, it helps if you draw your audience along your decision path with you – invite them to help you to solve the problem.

Impose a strict structure on your argument

> **Give them the necessary background**

'This is the situation we are in...'

---

* Antony Jay, in his excellent book *Effective Presentation* (Institute of Management/ Pitman publishing), offers this structure as 'a 6P alliterative mnemonic': Preface; Position; Problem; Possibilities; Proposal; Postscript'. In an earlier version of the book he limited himself to the middle four.

Show them that steps must be taken

'...and since we last met, interest rates have risen sharply...'

Present the options

'So you could ...'
'Or ...'
'Or ...'

Evaluate the options

'On grounds of economy...past experience...ethics...good taste... general prudence...a sense of adventure...'

Make your proposal

'The clear choice is...'

At each step in the process, your audience will be signalling agreement: 'Yes, we see how you reached this stage...yes, we follow your reasoning'.

That agreement with your logic is virtually the same as agreement with your proposal.

Build your structure close to your audience

The **evaluation** stage is vital; your audience must agree with your criteria.

If they have strong personal reasons for supporting one of your options, you cannot dismiss it casually:

> The idea of armed rebellion, comrade Guevara, we reject on grounds of common sense.

> We reject the idea that the earth revolves around the sun, signor Galilei, because it doesn't suit our theology.

While with other audiences, the criteria have to be weighted differently:

> We favour the bus over the train, Mr Getty, on the grounds that it is cheaper.

94\POWERFUL PRESENTATIONS

Exercise

Here are six reasons why your boss should read this book. Rank them in importance as they would appear to him.

1. Sometimes people go to sleep in his presentations.
2. He likes reading management books.
3. He has been promising himself a refresher course on 'Presentation skills'.
4. His visuals are dull and boring.
5. He is nervous about making presentations.
6. He has been making the same three presentations for years.

" I REALLY COULDN'T FOLLOW THE UNHAPPY ENDING; WHY DIDN'T HE JUST MARRY BOTH OF THEM? "

THE INTERNATIONAL ARENA

Gesture

If you naturally use your arms and hands when you speak, you are in danger of giving offence – or at least causing amusement – unintentionally.

One finger in the air ('Listen to this!') suggests the erect male organ in many parts of the world.

Elsewhere, forefinger and thumb closed in a circle ('Perfect!') signify the female pudenda.

When Margaret Thatcher won the battle for leadership of the Conservative Party, she gave the press a V-sign – back to front. Most people in the country received a clear message: this lady is so out of touch with the people, she doesn't realize that she's just told us all to F... off!

What this means to you

If you are making a presentation in some exotic spot – South of Milan or East of Vienna – don't jam your hands in your pockets for fear they will betray you.

Just keep your hands open and your fingers together, relaxed and slightly cupped – the way they hang when you let your arms droop by your side.

Now use these paddles for your gestures – pointing, beckoning, emphasizing.

Jokes

Jokes are very culture-specific.

Amusing anecdotes, a generally light-hearted attitude, funny pictures: these things travel quite well.

But if you have a store of Travelling Salesman funnies, or Shaggy Dog stories, or Bob Hope one-liners, leave them at home.

QUESTION AND ANSWER SESSION

We promised to return to the question of *competence* – letting your audience know that you are in command of your material and the overall situation. The best way to consolidate your position in their eyes is during the question and answer session.

HAVING THE RIGHT ATTITUDE

You have to work to build rapport with your audience; your presentation should not be like a monologue on the radio. (They might change stations.)

The participants on our training seminars accept the truth of this idea, and work hard to establish contact with their audiences during practice runs and rehearsals. They respond well to our coaching: '*Look* at the people!'; '*Involve* the people!'.

Yet many of them freeze, or turn in on themselves, when the audience fires questions at them – surely the ideal opportunity for some real, memorable dialogue!

Making a presentation is a stressful experience, and not least on a training course, where one is under particularly close scrutiny. The adrenalin 'high', produced during the performance, is poor preparation for a cosy Question-and-Answer session.

All too often, the response to the first question from the floor comes across as snappish: '17.5 per cent, obviously. I thought everybody knew that'; or impatient: 'The answer to that question was on the third graph I showed you'. And once a chilly atmosphere has settled over a Q & A forum, you can forget it.

Of course, you are different. You love being asked questions – especially under a spotlight. There are just one or two nagging doubts.

DEALING WITH THE DOUBTS

Expunge those inner voices that say:

'They'll ask me some bloody stupid question that has nothing to do with what I've been trying to demonstrate'

The questions they ask stem from their view of the situation. It is your job to help them to connect their view of the situation with your proposal.

If you didn't manage to show them that connection during the presentation, it's a good thing that this bloody stupid question has come up. It gives you the opportunity to try again.

'They'll ask me hostile questions to show I'm wrong'

Chapter 1 is about establishing yourself from the start as honest, and one of them.

If you have done that, and a hostile question then comes from an individual, you will at least know that the question stands out, to everybody present, as deliberately hostile. You can deal with it accordingly.

This does not mean fighting back. You are unlikely to win the hostile questioner over to your point of view, whatever you do. Say to yourself, 'The majority are on my side, and the best way to keep them there is to smile and answer gently'.

'They'll ask me difficult questions to show I don't know it all'

What honest person claims to know it all? You are not supposed to be a walking reference book.

If this really troubles you, make clear early in the presentation that there are limits to your competence. It will reinforce your image as an honest person.

Anyhow, you are always competent to say: 'I don't know, but I'll find out for you'.

'What if I can't hear the question?'

Ask him or her to repeat it. Better, ask him or her to frame it in a different way.

Either the speaker has a very weak voice, or you are having adrenalin trouble. The blood is still roaring in your ears.

'What if I mishear the question?'

If in doubt, repeat it back to check. Better, frame it in a different way yourself: 'I want to make sure I've got this right: you seem to be asking...'.

'What if the question is still incomprehensible?'

Ask the questioner to re-phrase it once more:

> I'm terribly sorry. Perhaps if you could approach it from another angle....

If it's still hopeless, say:

> That probably needs a proper conversation between us. After this session, perhaps? Meanwhile you have given me the opportunity to go a little deeper into one aspect....

'What if he or she is dissatisfied with my answer?'

First, find out: 'Does that answer your question?'

If the answer is No, then you have another opportunity to probe his interest and motivation: 'Perhaps if I had a better idea of why you ask this question...'.

GETTING READY

As with your presentation proper, the key to a good Q & A session is preparation.

A very clever, or very lucky, speaker can find a way to answer a question in a satisfactory way, *and* relate it back to his message, *and* use it as a step towards his objective.

This is hard to do on the fly, so make sure you...

Work out what their hot question is likely to be

You can often predict fairly accurately, and build a trailer into your main presentation:

> I won't dwell on the issue of x now; if any of you has a special interest, we can find time at the discussion stage....

Hook it back to your objective

Your answer must be of interest to the audience, but it should also underline your main message. Don't go as far as the politician who simply re-states his slogan and ignores the question entirely.

You don't have to be wonderfully subtle. Say:

> ...and if that answers your question, it also sheds further light on what we've seen throughout this discussion – namely that...

HOW SHOULD YOU BUILD AND DELIVER YOUR ARGUMENT?/99

Arm yourself with another two or three ways of stating your message

If you use the same turns of phrase over again, the audience becomes impatient. Ring the changes:

The rain in Spain stays mainly in the plain;

The lower lying parts of the peninsula enjoy most of the precipitation;

If you go to the mountains, don't expect more than the odd shower.

GETTING IT ROLLING

Ask yourself if they don't ask you

'So, are there any questions?' Silence. And the longer it goes on, the harder it becomes for anybody to produce a question.

So ask one yourself:

- ❑ any old question to get it rolling ('a colleague of mine was asked the other day...');
- ❑ a 'topical' question ('I heard some of you in the lobby discussing...and it strikes me that this raises a question appropriate to your circumstances');
- ❑ an 'urgent' question ('Your head of Human Resources kindly drove me here this evening, and he was very concerned about...'); or
- ❑ a 'probing' question ('I don't think I really did justice to the issue of rainfall over the Iberian flatlands...').

Very few listeners will remember later that it was you who asked the question; they will only remember your expert handling of it.

Plant a question in advance

Often, you can prime some member of the audience to ask you a good, juicy question at the start.

If several hands go up immediately when you invite questions, choose somebody else apart from your stooge. And when you do answer your stooge's question, don't go on too long, and don't deal with it exhaustively. You can expect a supplementary question....

HANDLING THE QUESTIONS

Your adrenalin is up, because you've just been performing – putting out. You are in the wrong state of mind for taking in; the risk is high that you will:

- simply respond to a trigger word in the question, and start to spout a lot of stuff that doesn't really help the questioner;
- talk too much; or
- create the wrong atmosphere – stress rather than relaxation.

How can you change gear?

Take your time

The audience will subconsciously recognize your predicament, and respect you if you say:

> Now let's pause for half a minute, while I get my breath back, and you think about what questions you might want to ask me.

You should use the time to calm yourself, and get ready to...

Embrace the question

Wrong:

- stand with one eyebrow raised ('I can't believe the naivety of this question!');
- sigh and turn away halfway through (I'm surrounded by idiots!');
- interrupt the questioner ('All right! All right! My time is precious!');
- produce a pat answer ('This is so easy, it's boring').

Much better:

- pay close attention, and signal courteous interest;
- pause, and let them see that you are thinking about the answer;
- replay the question, showing that you really want to get it right;

HOW SHOULD YOU BUILD AND DELIVER YOUR ARGUMENT?/101

- ❏ involve the whole audience, if your answer runs more than ten seconds – by sharing eye contact.

FINISHING WITH A BANG

If the question session comes at the end of your time slot, set up one final question which you can answer with great force.

Your audience is at the peak of alertness, so you can lodge a strong and positive impression of yourself and your message in their memories.

What this means to you

Approach the Question-and-Answer session as another opportunity to reinforce your message.

With that as your attitude, do a bit of homework and preparation.

Do everything you can to make communication clear and light during the session.

THE INTERNATIONAL ARENA

When you are working in English as the international business language, you can be straightforward with things like gratitude, flattery, and friendship.

Working within your own culture, you often rely on sub-verbal signals to transmit these messages. The English, for example, often find it a bit clumsy, or embarrassing, to say:

> You, of course, are an expert audience, well qualified to judge these matters for yourselves.

Yet this is just the sort of thing that you *should* say, if your audience is working in English-as-a-foreign language. They will not feel that you have overstated your point; such subtleties are generally suspended. They will be happy that you have expressed your positive emotions in a clear and sincere fashion.

The same applies when you are responding to questions. If an Englishman says to an English audience,

> That really is a fascinating question, and I am happy to do my best to answer it,

the audience might groan inwardly. Often it is considered more 'sophisticated' to leave this unsaid – to communicate *by tone of voice* that one is treating the question with respect.

Your international audience is not so good at reading tone of voice, or other implicit messages. Say it loud and clear:

What a useful question! Thank you very much!

A word of warning: don't 'give marks' to the questions you receive. If you say that the first one is '...a very good question', then the second might have to be 'excellent'. What mark do you give to Question Three?

YOUR DEMEANOUR

We have left to the last our suggestions about your demeanour. We say again: your audience will remember only a small part of what they hear, but a great deal of what they see. And a lot of what they see is you.

The way you look, the way you carry yourself, the expression on your face at key moments – these can enhance or destroy your message.

Often it would be quite wrong to state directly: 'I am a good person and you can depend on me', but you can send the signal loud and clear without speaking a word. In fact, you are doing it most of the time in your social and professional life; if you were transmitting other signals, you would be a flop in both departments. (Look at the teenagers you know: clumsy, shy, *gauche*, graceless, moody, self-centred, erratic, insensitive...and they can deliver all these messages just by the way they sit on a sofa.)

Yet we all experience stress when we have an audience staring at us, and that stress plays havoc with our body language. (We begin to appear clumsy, self-centred, insensitive...)

Adopt high status body language

This means:

❑ Not hiding – behind lecterns, tables or folded arms.

❑ Head up, shoulders back.

❑ Feet firmly planted, weight equally distributed.

❑ Arms relaxed at your sides, making gestures towards the audience, with fingers together and palms open.

Your base position should be something like that – your own version of stable equilibrium, with full exposure and contact.

> **Nothing to hide**
> **What you see is what you get**
> **Nothing up my sleeve**
> **Pleased to meet you.**

A lot of fidgety behaviour involves touching things, or parts of yourself – fiddling with notes, jingling keys in your pocket, scratching your nose, crossing and rubbing legs and feet together.

If you are prone to this, we offer one suggestion: get in touch with yourself in a way that your audience will not notice. You can try it now:

Make a circle of your thumb and middle finger, leaving the rest of your fingers relaxed. Now let that arm hang by your side. Quite unnoticeably, you can press finger and thumb hard together and work out all that tension.

Of course, a lot of fidgety behaviour is unconscious. This is where any good presentations training course will make use of video playbacks. You can arrange the experience – usually rather painful, but always fruitful – with a trusted friend, a camcorder, and a rehearsal.

Resist the temptation to try and rebuild your behaviour completely. Your audience will sense it if you try to become someone you are not, and all your efforts to project sincerity will produce the reverse effect – 'Who's he trying to fool?'

Rather, set yourself one target that you can achieve: I will stop tugging at my ear-lobe; I will smile more often.

Show, and use your eyes

The face is a wonderfully complex signalling system, and holds a supremely important position in human life. The mother's face is the baby's first object of study. Most banknotes carry a face. You could get the lettering or the geometrical patterns slightly wrong, and nobody would notice. But if your George Washington doesn't look like himself, your forged twenty-dollar bills will soon get you arrested.

Within the face, the eyes are crucial – especially for establishing trust. The poker face of the Mississippi steamboat cardsharp has dead eyes. The guilty man in the dock finds it hard to meet the eyes of his accuser.

Meet the eyes of your audience; let them look through the windows of your soul.

In a small group – up to say ten people – you can read a lot in your listeners' eyes.

If there are more than ten of them, you will not be able to give each individual his ration of eye contact. The trick then is to select, say, three people: one towards the left of the hall, one in the middle, and one to the right. One in the front row to chat to, one in the back row to project yourself at, one who will smile back at you and make you feel loved and wanted.

Everybody drops his gaze, or stares unfocused into the distance, when he is concentrating hard to retrieve facts or make calculations.

Exercise

Stare into the eyes of a friend, and recite the alphabet backwards without breaking eye contact. Very difficult.

Be conscious of this, and establish a rhythm in your speaking. Each time you reach the end of a 'paragraph' in your presentation, deliver the last idea, or sentence, looking directly into the eyes of one of your chosen recipients.

Then look at his eyes: are you getting feedback? If you find that he is asleep with his eyes open, that is valuable information. Time to do something about it.

Take your time

Too much chatter is seen as a sign of nervousness. It is also a sign that the presenter is overestimating his audience's mental capacities.

Picture this moment: a slide goes up on the screen. The speaker immediately interprets the data for his audience. He tells them they should try to remember it, and moves on to his next topic without a pause.

The audience does not read the slide. Nor do they listen to his interpretation. And so there is very little hope that they will remember either. They have been overloaded.

The normal brain can either read, or listen, or commit an item to memory; to do all three simultaneously is impossible. In these circumstances, the audience is likely to pass the time by sizing you up as a person – 'This speaker is in a great hurry/ nervous/ confused...'.

When you switch on a slide, or display a picture on the board, you will lose eye contact with your audience – turning to the visual material, and inviting them to do the same. At this moment, you should become inaudible and invisible for a while. Step away, lower your arms to your sides, go quiet, and use the quiet time to compose your thoughts.

What this means to you

Stand up straight, look them in the eyes, and take your time.

THE INTERNATIONAL ARENA

In certain cultures, it is inappropriate for a junior to display high status body language in front of his elders and betters.

If you are about to make a presentation in such an area, find a friendly native and ask about your standing in the eyes of your audience. You might have to practise a strong-but-humble posture.

Synopsis

If you have read this book from start to finish, you will be conscious of its deliberate structure – beginning with:

> **Your audience**

then addressing the nature of:

> **Your message**

and only then paying attention to:

> **You yourself.**

We firmly believe that this is the best order to work in when you are preparing a presentation.

Start by thinking hard about those who are to observe your performance. It is they who set the conditions and the limits for your material, and for your behaviour. Theirs is the important role; what happens in the minds and hearts of your listeners is paramount. You serve the audience and support that process.

Your objective should be firm and realistic; your message is the means of reaching that goal. The audience must surely influence your message, at the design stage. If you deliver the same message twice to different audiences, at least one of them has received imperfect service.

Further, when your performance begins, a very early task is to check: are these people really where you expected them to be? Are their levels of knowledge, their attitudes, their sense of humour all as you predicted? Make space for yourself to read their feedback signals, and modify your performance accordingly.

Let us imagine the work done on three levels:

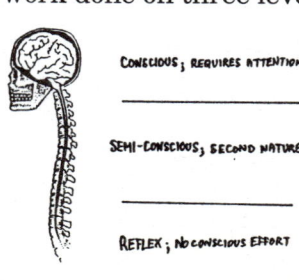

An average public speaker, who knows his material well, but is concerned about himself during his performance, arranges things like this:

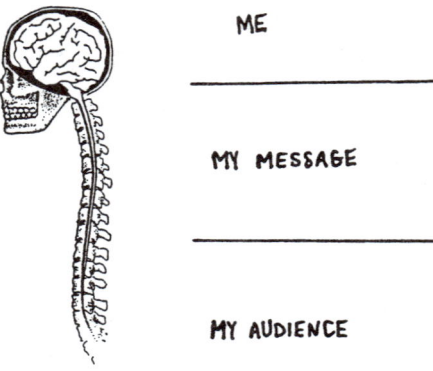

ME
———————
MY MESSAGE
———————
MY AUDIENCE

Look where that leaves the audience.

The truly successful speaker is the one who has managed to switch 'me' and 'my audience':

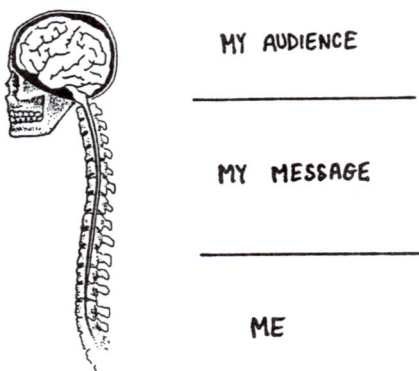

MY AUDIENCE
———————
MY MESSAGE
———————
ME

This apparently simple move separates the sheep from the goats. It demands empathy, training and practice.

What this means to you

You are already better than average as a presenter; you want to be excellent.

After every presentation you make, you re-live the occasion and criticize yourself constructively. Perhaps you are asking yourself:

- ❑ Did I handle my slides effectively?
- ❑ Did I cover the material with the right emphases?
- ❑ Did I demonstrate that I am competent?

These are all fine. But at this stage of your development, it is much more important to ask:

Did I observe audience reaction during the performance?

Was my performance influenced by what I observed?

Afterword

Apart from the overhead projector, most of what we have covered in this handbook would be familiar to Aristotle and Macaulay, as well as Mark Antony and Abraham Lincoln (*see* the appendices).

There is nothing new in any of this; we hope it has been a useful synthesis.

If you come up with something completely new in the field of communication and persuasion, you will make a mark in the world. Meanwhile, we suggest that you continue to borrow ideas from good speakers wherever you find them.

When you are faced with a choice between the elaborate and the simple, choose the latter. Finally, when all unnecessary clutter is stripped away, there are just your audience, your message and you.

What this means to you

Be an eclectic plagiarist; steal ideas from anywhere you like.

Be simple; be yourself.

A successful presentation creates wonders in the mind of your audience. These wonders take place when the audience accepts the idea which you are putting forward. If you look into their eyes, you can see it happen.

It is a fantastic experience.

Appendix 1

Mark Antony's oration

    Friends, Romans, countrymen, lend me your ears.
    I come to bury Caesar, not to praise him.
    The evil that men do lives after them;
    The good is oft interréd with their bones,
    So let it be with Caesar. The noble Brutus
    Hath told you Caesar was ambitious.
    If it were so, it was a grievous fault,
    And grievously hath Caesar answered it.
    Here, under leave of Brutus, and the rest, —
    For Brutus is an honourable man,
    So are they all; all honourable men, —
    Come I to speak in Caesar's funeral.
    He was my friend, faithful, and just to me;
    But Brutus says he was ambitious,
    And Brutus is an honourable man.
    He hath brought many captives home to Rome,
    Whose ransoms did the general coffers fill:
    Did this in Caesar seem ambitious?
    When that the poor have cried, Caesar hath wept.
    Ambition should be made of sterner stuff,
    Yet Brutus says he was ambitious,
    And Brutus is an honourable man.
    You all did see that, on the Lupercal,
    I thrice presented him a kingly crown,
    Which he did thrice refuse. Was this ambition?
    Yet Brutus says he was ambitious,
    And, sure, he is an honourable man.
    I speak not to disprove what Brutus spoke,
    But here I am, to speak what I do know.
    You all did love him once, not without cause;
    What cause witholds you then to mourn for him?
    O judgment! Thou art fled to brutish beasts,
    And men have lost their reason! Bear with me,

> My heart is in the coffin there with Caesar,
> And I must pause, till it come back to me.

The plebeians talk among themselves, agreeing with all Mark Antony's points so far. Recovering from his fit of stage grief, Antony then teases the audience with 'Caesar's will':

> Which, pardon me, I do not mean to read...

> You are not wood, you are not stones, but men;
> And being men, hearing the will of Caesar,
> It will inflame you, it will make you mad...

One more side-swipe at the conspirators,

> I fear I wrong the honourable men
> Whose daggers have stabbed Caesar....

Antony comes down from the pulpit, and makes his audience form a ring around him and Caesar's corpse:

> If you have tears, prepare to shed them now.
> You all do know this mantle. I remember
> The first time ever Caesar put it on.
> 'Twas on a summer's evening in his tent,
> That day he overcame the Nervii.
> Look, in this place ran Cassius' dagger through;
> See what a rent the envious Casca made;
> Through this, the well-belovéd Brutus stabbed,
> And, as he plucked his cursèd steel away,
> Mark how the blood of Caesar followed it...

> This was the most unkindest cut of all....

The plebeians start shouting for revenge.

> Good friends, sweet friends, let me not stir you up
> To such a sudden flood of mutiny....

> I come not, friends, to steal away your hearts;
> I am no orator, as Brutus is.
> But, as you know me all, a plain blunt man
> That love my friend...

> ...I only speak right on.
> I tell you that which you yourselves do know,
> Show you sweet Caesar's wounds, poor, poor dumb mouths,
> And bid them speak for me; But were I Brutus,

> And Brutus Antony, there were an Antony
> Would ruffle up your spirits, and put a tongue
> In every wound of Caesar, that should move
> The stones of Rome to rise and mutiny.
>
> *All*: We'll mutiny.

Finally, Antony pulls them back from the brink to read out Caesar's will, leaving to the people all his walks,

> His private arbours and new-planted orchards,
> On this side Tiber....

Then he turns the mob loose to run riot.

Appendix 2

Lincoln's Gettysburg Address

Fourscore and seven years ago our fathers brought forth on this continent a new nation, conceived in liberty and dedicated to the proposition that all men are created equal.

Now we are engaged in a great civil war, testing whether that nation or any nation so conceived and so dedicated can long endure. We are met on a great battlefield of that war. We have come to dedicate a portion of that field as a final resting-place for those who here gave their lives that that nation might live. It is altogether fitting and proper that we should do this. But in a larger sense, we cannot dedicate, we cannot consecrate, we cannot hallow this ground. The brave men, living and dead who struggled here have consecrated it far above our poor power to add or detract. The world will little note nor long remember what we say here, but it can never forget what they did here. It is for us the living rather to be dedicated here to the unfinished work which they who fought here have thus far so nobly advanced. It is rather for us to be here dedicated to the great task remaining before us – that from these honored dead we take increased devotion to that cause for which they gave us the last full measure of devotion – that we here highly resolve that these dead shall not have died in vain, that this nation under God shall have a new birth of freedom, and that government of the people, by the people, for the people shall not perish from the earth.